This text provides clinicians with a comprehensive guide for working with autistic children and their families. It offers practical assistance with early diagnosis, cutting-edge treatment options and goals, interdisciplinary insights, and available resources. Empirical research findings are presented in a clear, accessible manner. Perhaps most importantly, vivid case examples bring both the therapist's and patient's experience to the fore as they work towards recovery.

This clear and informative book should be required reading for professionals and students in the fields of medicine, social work, psychology, education, and any other clinicians who work with children on the autism spectrum.

Jennifer Hillman, PhD, is a licensed clinical Psychologist and Associate Professor of Psychology at The Pennsylvania State University, Berks College.

Stephen Snyder is a Senior Lecturer in English at The Pennsylvania State University, Berks College.

James Neubrander, MD, is a board certified diplomat in environmental medicine. He is a member of the think tank of the internationally recognized Autism Research Institute.

Childhood Autism

A Clinician's Guide to Early Diagnosis and Integrated Treatment

Jennifer Hillman and Stephen Snyder with James Neubrander

Routledge
Taylor & Francis Group

LONDON AND NEW YORK

First published 2007
by Routledge
27 Church Road, Hove, East Sussex BN3 2FA

Simultaneously published in the USA and Canada
by Routledge
270 Madison Avenue, New York, NY 10016

Routledge is an imprint of the Taylor & Francis Group, an Informa
business

Typeset by Regent Typesetting
Printed and bound in Great Britain by TJ International Ltd,
Padstow, Cornwall
Paperback cover design by Anú Design

This publication has been produced with paper manufactured
to strict environmental standards and with pulp derived from
sustainable forests.

British Library Cataloguing in Publication Data
A catalogue record for this book is available from the British
Library

Library of Congress Cataloging in Publication Data
Hillman, Jennifer L.
    Childhood autism : a clinician's guide to early diagnosis and
integrated treatment / Jennifer Hillman and Stephen Snyder with
James Neubrander.
        p. ; cm.
    Includes bibliographical references and index.
    ISBN-13: 978-0-415-37259-6 (hardback)
    ISBN-10: 0-415-37259-3 (hardback)
    ISBN-13: 978-0-415-37260-2 (pbk.)
    ISBN-10: 0-415-37260-7 (pbk.)
    1. Autism in children. I. Snyder, Stephen, 1967- II. Neubrander,
James, 1949- III. Title.
    [DNLM: 1. Autistic Disorder--diagnosis. 2. Autistic Disorder-
-therapy. 3. Autistic Disorder--psychology. 4. Child. 5. Early
Diagnosis. 6. Education, Special. WM 203.5 H654c 2007]
    RJ506.A9C445 2007
    618.92'85882--dc22
                                2006024242

ISBN: 978-0-415-37259-6 (hbk)
ISBN: 978-0-415-37260-2 (pbk)

For Sean

Contents

Acknowledgments

This book would not have been possible without the help, support, and professional expertise of so many. We are indebted to the countless numbers of children and family members affected by autism who were willing to share their experience and stories, and we would like to thank a number of people, including George Stricker, Romain Jensen, Eric Fisher, Sherry Mierhoff, Patricia Barnes, Molly Dallmeyer, Stephanie Padgett, Daniele Richards, Rowena Fantasia-Davis, Donna Chimera, Patrick Ross, Rick Zweig, Michael Bibbo, Eileen Rosendahl, Greg Hinrichsen, Christine Li, Jeffrey Bradstreet, Thomas Skoloda, Lawrence Miller, John and Pam Lane, David Nicodemis, Cheryl Gustitis, members of the Berks County, Pennsylvania chapter of the ASA, the informal parent group at Health South Rehabilitation Hospital in Reading, PA, and Ken Fifer and our very supportive colleagues at Penn State Berks, among others. We are also grateful for Joanne Forshaw, our editor at Routledge, and our thoughtful reviewers. And certainly this book would not have been possible without the generous love and support of our families.
JH & SS

Foreword

Temple Grandin, Ph.D.,
Best-selling author of *Thinking in Pictures*
and *Animals in Translation*

When I was a child, I was severely autistic. I was lucky that a wise neurologist named Dr. Bronson Cruthers referred my mother to an excellent speech therapist who used many ABA (Applied Behavior Analysis) methods. Mrs. Reynolds was one of those experienced teachers who knew how to be gently insistent. If she pushed me too hard I would have a tantrum, and if she did not push at all I made no progress. I have observed that good teachers use the same methods regardless of the program they are using. As a clinician, you will observe that some teachers develop a "knack" for working with a particular child and others may not. If little progress is being made, a different teacher may be more effective with that child.

The most common mistake that teachers make is to drive the child into sensory overload. When I was little, loud noises such as the school bell hurt my ears like a dentist's drill hitting a nerve. For another child, a gentle touch might hurt. Most children with autism will make better progress if teaching is done in a quiet room that has no fluorescent lights. Fluorescent lights bother some children because they make the room flicker like a disco. Use standard incandescent light bulbs. The degree of sensory oversensitivity will vary greatly from case to case. In the more severe children, a busy, crowded supermarket may trigger non-stop tantrums. This occurs because the child feels like he is inside both the light show and speakers at a rock concert.

Children who cannot tolerate a normal classroom or shopping mall are often not able to process both auditory information and visual information at the same time. They are mono-channel. They either have to listen to something or look at it. Sometimes they respond best if the teacher uses a very soft voice. Another problem they may have is that they are not able to hear hard consonant sounds easily. Even though they pass the pure tone hearing test they may be hearing vowels with no consonants. My speech teacher helped me by stretching out and enunciating consonants. She would hold up a cup and say "cc u pp." When I was four I could understand adults when they spoke directly to me, but when the grown-ups talked rapidly to each other it sounded like gibberish. I thought the grown-ups had a special adult language. Teachers and therapists working with autistic children need to understand problems with sensory processing and oversensitivity. I strongly recommend that clinicians read books written by people on the autism spectrum. This will provide a better understanding of what it is like to have a sensory system that is malfunctioning.

Childhood Autism provides both practical and scientific information on different therapies for young children with autism. It will be most useful for clinicians who will be working with newly diagnosed children. One thing I really liked about this book was its open-minded approach to different types of therapies. Each type of therapy is examined in a clear manner without a lot of scientific jargon. Along with the scientific information, it includes quotes from individuals on the spectrum and case histories. This will provide insight from both individuals with autism and their parents. Different subjects such as helping parents deal with the strain on the marriage and finances are also included. Asperger's syndrome and milder disorders in which language is not delayed are not covered. *Childhood Autism* will be very useful for teachers, psychologists and other therapists who are entering the field of autism, and the information in it will be extremely useful for therapists and teachers who work with young children on the more severe end of the spectrum.

Chapter 1

Introduction

One out of 166 children in the United States receives a diagnosis of autism or an autism spectrum disorder.

The number of children formally diagnosed with autism has been rising steadily over the past twenty years. In the early 1980s, approximately 1 in 5,000 children were diagnosed with autism. At the turn of the century, 1 in 500 received a diagnosis, and current figures indicate that 1 out of 166 children in the United States receives a formal diagnosis of autism or an autism spectrum disorder (Chakrabarti & Fombonne, 2001; Strock, 2004). Although there is no formal reporting center in the UK, recent estimates suggest that 1 out of 170 children are diagnosed with autism there (Chakrabarti & Fombonne, 2005). When autism first emerged as a clinical disorder among children, Bruno Bettelheim posited that "refrigerator mothers," so named for their chilly disposition, actually caused their children to become sick. This misunderstanding continued for decades until Bernie Rimland, M.D. suspected specific neurological and biological imbalances as a cause of autism (e.g., Edelson & Rimland, 2003), and parents were no longer "blamed" for their child's illness.

Despite this forward thinking, however, patients and their families still face significant problems when coping with the devastating effects of childhood autism. Many children suffering from autism receive little or no empirically supported treatment, and the average age of diagnosis hovers around five years of age, though many experts believe that early intervention should begin much sooner (Strock, 2004). Private insurance typically fails to cover related treatments, whether they are evidence-based or not. Recent studies also suggest that parents of children diagnosed with autism are more likely to be depressed, and more likely to be severely depressed (Bitsika & Sharpley, 2004), than parents of children diagnosed with cancer (Hughes & Lieberman, 1990).

When asked about her experience in psychotherapy as a mother of a four-year-old son with autism, Mary, a 34-year-old ER physician assistant, crossed her arms and snorted,

> Well, you know I just couldn't believe it when my therapist had the nerve to say to me, "Well, you know, all parents worry about their children. What you are going through really isn't that different from what all other parents are going through." I wanted to say to her, "Well, isn't that rich. Maybe you're worried about whether your kid is going to get into the right college, find a job, stay away from drugs, have a girlfriend, or fall off the monkey bars. I'm worried about whether my five-year-old kid is going to ever speak instead of scream, look at me and say, 'I love you' or even 'Want juice,' play with a toy, or go through life at the complete mercy of others if something ever happens to me. It sure as hell would be nice to have a kid who you could get someone to baby-sit for. But right now I'm most concerned about when my kid is going to stop wearing diapers and pooping in his pants." She just didn't get it [the day-to-day experience of a parent and child living with autism] at all.

Unfortunately, Mary's experience may not be that unusual. Limited training is available to psychologists and other mental healthcare providers regarding cutting-edge, empirically supported treatments for this developmental disorder, as well as for assistance in managing the often challenging countertransference encountered in treatment.

This text is designed to provide psychologists and other mental healthcare providers with a basic guide for working with children and their families who are suffering, or are suspected to be suffering, from autism. The goal of this book is to provide assistance with differential diagnoses, treatment options and goals, interdisciplinary insights, and a variety of clinical resources. (Although significant attention can and should be paid to the controversial etiology of autism spectrum disorders, including the role of environmental neurotoxins such as mercury and pesticides, this text is limited to a discussion of diagnosis and treatment.) Empirical research findings related to early diagnostic features and warning signs, and new and established modes of treatment, will be presented in a clear, concise, and reader-friendly manner. Suggestions also will be made to help therapists cope with often challenging emotional aspects of diagnosis and treatment with these children and their families. And perhaps even more importantly, vivid case examples will be provided to bring the experience of the therapists, affected family members, and children themselves to the fore as they work toward symptom reduction or remission.

Another critical aspect of this text is its focus upon interdisciplinary treatment. Autism is a multifaceted disorder that encompasses neurological problems, social and interpersonal problems, biomedical issues, family systems problems, school-based considerations, sensory dysfunction, financial considerations, and public policy issues. Also, because of the text's emphasis upon a timely diagnosis followed by a requisite, interdisciplinary treatment plan, it is well suited for a variety of mental health professionals and individuals who work directly with children, including psychologists, psychiatrists, social workers, counselors, occupational therapists, physical therapists, teachers, school administrators, pastors and other religious figures. Although this book is designed for mental healthcare providers, it is quite suitable for the generalist practitioner as well as the child specialist.

Each chapter of the text will be introduced here to provide readers with a comprehensive overview. Chapter 2 is designed to delineate and illustrate the primary diagnostic feature of autism and Pervasive Developmental Disorder, not otherwise specified (PDD-NOS), and to introduce research that promotes early detection of various behavioral symptoms. Significant advances in research suggest that many children with autism can receive a diagnosis as early as one year of age (see Goin and Myers, 2004, for a review) and benefit significantly from early intervention (Eaves & Ho, 2004). A key feature of this chapter is an outline of the essential components of a patient screening and a comprehensive diagnostic assessment for the presence of autism.

The core features of autism, including significant deficits in verbal and nonverbal communication, as well as the presence of stereotypical, nonfunctional behavior, will be presented. Case studies and clinical anecdotes will illustrate aspects of "stimming" (i.e., repetitive, self-stimulatory behavior), echolalia, insistence upon sameness, treating others as objects, inappropriate affective displays, and sensory defensiveness. To provide clinicians with an additional frame of reference, comparisons between the behavior of a child with autism and that of a typically developing peer will be offered. Autism *per se* will be discussed as a point along a diagnostic continuum. Myths in which many people assume that autism is synonymous with the presence of mental retardation and splinter skills will be debunked, and the importance of ruling out genetic disorders, such as Rett's disease, and medical disorders, such as seizures, will be emphasized.

Another unique feature of this chapter will be its discussion of the challenges that therapists face as they work with parents to determine whether or not their child has a serious developmental disorder. Common experiences among therapists include denial, sadness, and anger, as well as feelings of confusion when attempting to identify appropriate resources and tools for assessment. The case example of one psychologist who delayed the appropriate diagnosis and treatment of one patient's child for approximately six months, and who later recognized and processed her countertransference, will be presented as a valuable tool, among others, for learning.

Although all children with autism are strikingly different, one may wonder, "What is a typical day like for a child with autism?" Chapter 3 is designed to give therapists a better sense of the internal experience of children suffering from autism. Case examples and commentary from young adults diagnosed with autism will be offered to provide an awareness of the often surprisingly different internal experience and attributions made by individuals on the spectrum. For example, some young adults with autism describe being touched or bumped gently as extremely unpleasant, to the point where they feel like they are being scratched with sandpaper or even burned. Such therapeutic insights can help depressed or anxious parents make better attributions for their autistic child's behavior, and aid in developing more effective treatment plans. Practitioners will be cautioned that every child has a different internal experience and that individualized communication with and observation of patients takes clear priority.

This chapter is also designed to help therapists better treat parents who commonly experience post-traumatic stress disorder, depression, anxiety, marital problems, and substance abuse at various stages in their child's diagnosis and treatment. In other words, therapists must treat the entire family and not simply the identified patient. Pros and cons of the Treatment and Education of Autistic and related Communication Handicapped Children (TEACCH) program, in which parents are instructed to take a primary role in their child's treatment, will be discussed. Clinicians can recognize the parents' expanding roles as parent, teacher, advocate, nurse, occupational therapist, disciplinarian, financial advisor, caregiver, and researcher. Therapists can also provide essential guidance in time management, anger management, and the ability to tolerate ambiguity. The value of couples therapy, and the unique dynamic that often develops between a parent who spends more time at work and a parent who provides more of the child's direct care will be presented as well.

Practitioners will be made aware of the challenges inherent in working with children with autism. Insurance coverage may be limited, and an extensive, integrative approach is almost certainly required for effective intervention. Work with a mute, physically aggressive child may require a specific behavioral approach, whereas work with a child's depressed parent may be best suited for insight-oriented talk therapy. And, therapeutic intervention with a family, including parents and neurotypical (NT) siblings, may call for yet another, different systems approach. Clinicians must become comfortable with shifting back and forth between advocacy, primary care, and eclectic forms of therapy. Knowledge of current, empirically supported research is required, as well as an ability to work well with other healthcare professionals.

In Chapter 4, the vital history of Applied Behavioral Analysis (ABA), an intensive one-on-one behavioral therapy, will be covered, along with a detailed review of operant and classical conditioning as applied to autism and ABA in particular. This includes the pros and cons of traditional ABA, such as the sometimes robot-like speech and limited interests in social interaction and spontaneous play. (Some parents who apply strict ABA principles note, "Sandra is more likely to talk or play when she's sitting at her little desk, or when she knows the therapist is around.") Because ABA represents in-vivo therapy, many generalist psychologists and therapists may not be able to engage in such extensive treatment with a child, but they may find themselves helping parents gather the appropriate behavioral specialists and therapeutic support staff and helping to oversee a program that includes realistic goals and data collection.

The use of ABA and modified ABA represents the foundation of an effective, empirically supported treatment program, and it can help children learn to speak, use the toilet, anticipate activities for the day, and reduce self-injurious and self-stimulatory behavior. Parents also can be taught that echolalia and other negative symptoms can be used as stepping stones in order to get a child to engage in meaningful speech. (The introduction of pictorially based systems as a temporary substitute for language among severely affected children will also be discussed.) The appropriate use of reinforcers in a modified ABA program can help make language useful and fun, rather than a robot-like chore.

Chapter 5 provides critical information about many of the movement and sensory related disorders experienced by children suffering from autism. A core diagnostic feature for children with autism is their apparent inability to play. When observed at a school or neighborhood playground, many children diagnosed with autism will run or walk repetitively along the perimeter of the playground and do not even attempt to play on the slide, swings, or merry-go-round. Recent evidence suggests that this apparent inability to play is linked not with mental retardation or some other kind of cognitive deficit, or even with a general disinterest in functional play, but with an underlying, physical inability to move one's body through space. Ataxia and related sensory impairments, also called problems with sensory integration (SI), are often associated with an autistic child's inability to color with crayons, play catch, or to steady the self enough to climb a slide.

Obtaining an appropriate diagnosis and treatment from occupational and physical therapists will significantly improve the likelihood that these children will benefit from psychologically based approaches to treatment. The skills learned in occupational therapy, which may include riding a bike, playing catch, becoming proficient with a computer mouse, or self-dressing, can be used as reinforcers in ABA programs, decrease anxiety and frustration in children, and help families increase their leisure time together. Clinicians also will be informed about specific warning signs for such neurological dysfunction (e.g., constant falls, walking against walls, staring sideways at lines and corners). An understanding of many patients' unusual perceptual experiences can also help therapists address a variety of problem behaviors, ranging from fighting with other children to fear of vacuum cleaners and hair dryers. Systematic desensitization, much like that used among individuals suffering from phobias or obsessive-compulsive behavior, can be surprisingly effective.

Chapter 6 addresses some of the most important, emergent work in the field of autism, namely the development of various programs and therapies designed to increase child-driven social interaction and communication. Although limited empirical research is currently available to support its use, enough anecdotal evidence exists to warrant its review. One of the core behavioral symptoms in autism is a deficit in social skills, based largely upon serious limitations in spontaneous, combined attention and social referencing. Brain imagery analyses suggest that children with autism do not respond to typical, innate social cues for mutual eye gaze or pointing, even at a very early age. Social skills programs such as Relationship Development Intervention (RDI), pioneered by Steven Gutstein (2000), incorporate behavioral principles as a way to help children learn to spontaneously seek out and receive reinforcement when they engage in joint attention and social referencing.

Other important issues related to social skills acquisition include the pros and cons of scheduling therapeutic play dates with typical peers or other children on the spectrum, and whether to pair children with similar or dissimilar skills. Some research suggests that children with autism who have the ability to imitate may acquire valuable skills and habits from interacting with neurotypical peers, whereas other research suggests that children matched with higher functioning children do not learn functional social skills because the advanced children alter their behavior to adapt to the needs of the child with autism. Options for offering therapeutic social groups that incorporate small groups of children on the spectrum with psychologists, speech therapists, and occupational therapists are included. Because of the typical lack of therapeutic services available in most communities, some psychologists have created niche practices around such small group therapy sessions. Although the greatest ambiguity exists regarding the effectiveness of social skills "training," it remains one of the most important areas for intervention.

A wealth of evidence is mounting that autism, like schizophrenia and bipolar disorder, has a biomedical component. One goal of Chapter 7 is to help practitioners realize that, as an ethical practitioner, one must become aware of the inherent relationship between psychological and biomedical problems in autism. For example, increasing evidence suggests that many problem behaviors observed among children with autism (e.g., violent tantrums; self-injurious behavior; refusal to use the bathroom) are directly related to the presence of underlying chronic pain (Afzal *et al.*, 2003) and an inability to communicate about that pain. Estimates suggest that up to 50 percent of children with autism suffer from painful, chronic constipation, undiagnosed colitis (Melmed, Schneider, Fabes, Philips, & Reichelt, 2000), food and environmental allergies, and ear or yeast infections (Edelson & Rimland, 2003; McCandless, 2003). This chapter will introduce some of the biomedical problems that children with autism typically possess, and highlight how critical it is to manage a child's pain and discomfort. If a child is in significant physical distress, even the best therapist, teacher, or other mental health provider is going to encounter significant difficulty accomplishing goals in treatment. In essence, an interdisciplinary approach to diagnosis and treatment becomes essential.

Another unfortunate aspect of autism is that many children have specific diets or dietary restrictions. Many children with autism have problems eating a variety of foods, for reasons that remain unclear at time of writing. Chapter 7 will present information about eating programs, in which behavioral principles are used to introduce children to a variety of food. Still another unfortunate, common experience for children with autism and their families is the need for a significant number of medical procedures. Many patients require frequent blood draws, injections, colonoscopies, or other invasive procedures. Even going to the dentist for a general cleaning and exam can be challenging. Based upon a collection of research in pain management and behavior therapy, specific suggestions are offered so that mental health practitioners can help parents and children prepare for and cope with such medical procedures. Additional guidelines will be offered to help therapists empower parents to communicate more effectively with physicians and other healthcare professionals.

As highlighted in Chapter 8, when children suffering from autism enter the school system, practitioners must work closely with patients and their families to help foster a smooth transition. The challenges are great; children who are typically resistant to change must become familiar with an entirely new set of professionals and physical surroundings. All children who wish to receive specialized educational services must obtain an Individualized Educational Plan (IEP) from their school, which requires extended interactions with and evaluations by school psychologists, administrators, occupational therapists, and speech therapists. This process can be overwhelming for both children and their parents. Therapists must become familiar with various legal terms, and can support parents as they make difficult decisions about inclusion, the presence of individual aides, and resource rooms.

A number of children who enjoy progress in ABA home-based or clinic programs experience significant regression after they enter a public school setting with an unfamiliar physical environment, an entirely new population of students, and a higher student-to-teacher ratio. Therapists must be aware of this potential barrier to continued therapeutic progress, and work closely with families to make the transition as smooth as possible. Therapists can assist families throughout this process in a variety of ways. Many can serve as advocates or essential sources of information to parents about basic issues of diagnosis and testing. This chapter will also review and critique some general assessment instruments for autism often used in school-based evaluations.

Chapter 9 will present cutting-edge research that offers therapists information about the actual brainwaves emitted by children suffering from autism. Emergent research on QEEG patterns suggests that when compared to neurotypical peers, children diagnosed with autism are significantly more likely to produce theta and delta, than alpha and beta, brainwaves. It is interesting to note that the presence of theta waves and delta waves is consistent with seizure activity, a diagnosis of attention deficit disorder, and the presence of sleep. In other words, when children with autism appear to be staring into space, disinterested in people and things around them, their brains may be sending them the message to "sleep."

Related findings will be presented about developments in neurofeedback (NF), a specialized form of biofeedback, in which children as young as three years of age have been taught to monitor and shift their brainwaves to more desirable, daytime frequencies. Other types of treatment, including the use of music therapy, animal assisted or pet therapy, art therapy and individual psychotherapy will be reviewed. Therapists will be cautioned that some of these interventions have accumulated more empirical support than others, but that their use in individual treatment plans can be explored carefully on a case-by-case basis. In other words, most research suggests that virtually all effective treatments for children with autism involve intensive, one-on-one contact or involvement, and clinical practice suggests that every child must be evaluated individually in order to select the best treatment.

This chapter is also designed to help therapists enable parents to deal better with a constant level of uncertainty in their lives, and to foster a sense of resiliency and hope for the future. In addition, some attention will be given to the controversy over recovery versus remission. Some experts argue that autism represents a chronic condition, whereas others assert that the brain is plastic enough to experience and maintain long-term change. Many therapists find that patients don't really worry about the name given to these changes, as long as they are positive. Research on resiliency, humor, and coping strategies will be reviewed in order to help therapists guide families in maintaining a sense of hope and purpose. And because the ability to ascribe meaning to a challenging or traumatic situation can often promote positive outcomes for all family members involved, the often underutilized role of grandparents will also be explored.

Another fundamental factor for family members often involves the myriad of choices available for treatment – some of which sound too good to be true. Many parents are justifiably desperate to do or try anything to help their child, or even communicate or bond with them on a very basic level. For parents who do not have a background in the social sciences, medicine, or research methods, very difficult choices must be made in the absence of general information about empirical efficacy. For example, some individuals promoting a specific treatment may promise a 90 percent success rate and, in the absence of any controlled research or empirical data, provide dramatic testimonials in which parents describe a child who suddenly learns to say, "I love you, Mom! Thanks for never giving up on me," or some other variant. It becomes critical to educate parents about experimental design, including areas of concern such as small sample sizes and biased observers. In other words, treatments that promise exceptional results based upon their implementation with only a handful of children, and determined only by subjective reports from the treatment providers themselves, are questionable. Some therapies that require thousands of dollars and specialized, certified consultants or training programs, that maintain secretive protocols unavailable to the general public or available for review by other professionals, may also be suspect.

It is not a therapist's job to persuade a family to adopt or reject any specific treatment, but to help them make an informed decision based upon available information and research principles. Thus, some family members may choose to be more conservative and not to engage in any treatment unless it has been validated in peer-reviewed journals and can be considered evidence-based. However, because developmental research is fraught with inherent challenges and is difficult to conduct in traditional, double-blind studies, other families may adopt the more liberal stance in which they will consider virtually any therapy or treatment as long as it does not cause harm to their child or cost an exorbitant amount of money. Every family is different, and therapists can help parents who may have differing viewpoints communicate better with each other, and with the related treatment professionals, about expected outcomes.

When exploring a new treatment, therapists can help parents attempt to evaluate its outcome more objectively. For example, when initiating a new behavioral therapy (or any other intervention), parents may be advised to consider not telling other teachers, professionals or caregivers who work with their child about the new treatment to see if they spontaneously report any improvement or regression. Therapists can also help parents understand that when introducing more than one new treatment at a time, it becomes virtually impossible to discern the true effectiveness of either individual treatment. Therapists can then help families decide for themselves if they want to institute a number of changes at once, in the interest of time, or to take a slower approach. As one mother of a five-year-old with autism noted, however, "Justin doesn't have a lot of time to waste. Every day he stays trapped in his own little world, he misses out. I've got to put some of my questions about which therapy works better than another aside and just go for it." In many cases, therapists can help parents identify and separate powerful emotions from factual knowledge in order to make the final treatment determination that is right for their child and their family.

While the controversial etiology of autism is generally not discussed in this text to place greater emphasis upon early diagnosis and treatment, the authors wish to emphasize the critical role of a comprehensive medical assessment for each affected child. As noted in Chapter 7, many children with autism suffer from undiagnosed chronic pain, underlying infections, allergies, nutritional deficiencies, and immune system dysfunction. Screening for the presence of environmental toxins may also be considered. (The Defeat Autism Now! organization can be a valuable, overall resource for professionals and parents.) In essence, no matter what "caused" a child's autism, an integrated approach to treatment remains essential.

For the most part, this text will focus upon children suffering from autism or PDD-NOS rather than Asperger's disorder. Diagnostic criteria for Asperger's disorder (American Psychiatric Association, 2000) are similar to those of autism in terms of significant impairment in social interaction and the presence of restrictive and stereotyped patterns of behavior, interests, and activities. However, the primary distinction between the two is that children with Asperger's disorder develop language normally (e.g., use single words by age two and simple phrases by age three). These children are also identified as having no clinically significant delays in cognitive development or self-help skills. Clinically, children with Asperger's disorder often appear like bright "little professors" or "know it alls" because they spout knowledge, trivia, or instructions at will (e.g., information on washing machines, street signs, birthdays of famous people), often with complete disregard for the interest level of those around them. Many of these boys and girls appear oblivious to the disinterest of those around them and continue with their monologues or become angry when others show disdain or boredom with their specific topic of choice. Consider one seven-year-old boy with Asperger's disorder who stated, "I don't understand why people don't want to hear about my bolt collection. I just don't get it!" In other words, although these children are often adept with the semantics of language, they have significant difficulties in using language to foster or sustain meaningful social interactions. However, because many clinicians regard Asperger's disorder as being located on the same diagnostic continuum with autism and PDD-NOS, many of the recommendations and guidelines in this text will certainly apply.

Another limitation of this book is its emphasis upon autism among children rather than upon adolescents and adults. Although a number of treatment programs and research projects now focus upon the diagnosis and treatment of childhood autism, notably less attention appears to be paid to teenagers and adults with the same diagnosis. Unfortunately, many parents comment upon the sudden dearth of services available when their child enters high school or college. If a child does achieve enough success to enter a college, entirely new rules and regulations exist regarding the provision of special services. The vast majority of states in the US also fail to provide any kind of subsidized treatment or assistance for adults suffering from autism once they leave the public school system. Thus, clinicians, researchers, and public policy makers must be encouraged to exert significantly greater time, focus, and resources upon this expanding patient population.

This book is probably one third the length of what it could be. It is difficult to winnow down the requisite information, especially when readers can benefit from the inclusion of multiple case examples. In many ways, autism is an elusive disorder, and its symptom presentation varies greatly among different children. With the help of practitioners from a variety of professions, such children are more likely to achieve better clinical outcomes. To begin to understand autism and recognize its many variations, clinicians must often spend countless hours with many different children and their families. Hopefully, this text will empower clinicians to begin work with this critically important patient group, expand their professional repertoire to include collaboration with practitioners from a variety of disciplines, or seek out additional professional resources or training. All children with autism deserve the very best clinical care and attention. As noted by one adult diagnosed with autism, "When I think back to when I was a kid, it made the most difference to me when someone was just patient, and they took the time to really be with me." Thus, clinicians can be advised to place their primary emphasis upon attempts to understand the child's experience.

Chapter 2

Making an accurate and timely diagnosis

> I knew something was wrong with Jason by the time he was two. But everyone told me to wait it out, that all kids are different, that boys always mature later than girls. I sometimes sit and wonder how much better he would be doing right now if someone had actually listened to me instead of treating me like a crazy, overprotective mother, and he got the right diagnosis and treatment sooner.
>
> – Mother of Jason, diagnosed with autism at age four

Exciting advances suggest that clinically significant warning signs for autism can be detected as early as 12 months of age. Because early intervention is so critical, it is essential that practitioners become familiar with general diagnostic criteria for autism, as well as newly available screening instruments and plans for a comprehensive diagnostic assessment. Despite a number of advances in the field, no single physiological marker or blood test is available for making a diagnosis; the focus is entirely upon a child's observable behavior. It is also interesting to note that autism is four times more likely to be diagnosed in boys than in girls. Any discussion of diagnostic criteria for autism, therefore, must begin with a perfunctory review of the DSM-IV-TR (2000) of the American Psychiatric Association, used concurrently by mental and medical health professionals. Autistic disorder is listed as one of five pervasive developmental disorders including autistic disorder, Rett's disorder, childhood disintegrative disorder, Asperger's disorder, and pervasive developmental disorder not otherwise specified (PDD-NOS or simply PDD).

A diagnosis of autism (or PDD) comes with significant consequences. With such a diagnosis, subsequent insurance claims may be accepted or denied, and many insurance companies claim that autism or any other developmental disorder is chronic and untreatable, and thus a non-reimbursable, disorder. School districts may be required to provide various services depending upon a child's diagnosis. Parents may emerge from a previous state of denial about their child's condition or may revert into a state of depression. Teachers may regard a child as unique or as a significant problem, and the child, if significantly self-aware, may develop an impaired self-image or be motivated to engage in behaviors more like NT children around him. In essence, making an accurate diagnosis is a serious proposition that demands serious consideration, especially when it is a key factor in obtaining essential, early intervention.

DIAGNOSTIC CRITERIA

To meet criteria for a diagnosis of autism as articulated in the DSM-IV-TR (APA, 2000), by the age of three, a child must display a developmental delay or abnormal functioning in one or more of the following: (1) social interaction; (2) language in relation to the facilitation of social interaction; and (3) imaginative or pretend play. Moreover, these deficits cannot be accounted for by other disorders, such as Rett's Disorder or Childhood Disintegrative Disorder. In addition, a child must display at least two or more of the following symptoms of social impairment: (1) limited use of nonverbal behaviors, such as eye-to-eye gaze (eye contact), appropriate facial expressions, and gestures to regulate social interaction; (2) lack of peer relationships at the appropriate developmental level; (3) absence of spontaneous sharing of experience via showing, bringing, or pointing out objects of interest; (4) lack of emotional or social reciprocity.

A child must also show impairment in communication as manifested by at least one of the following: a delay or total lack of spoken language development (if a child attempts to point or gesture instead, this criterion is not met); (2) an inability to start or maintain a conversation with others; (3) stereotyped or repetitive use of language or idiosyncratic language; and (4) an absence of spontaneous make-believe or pretend play, particularly in a social context. A child must also display at least one of the following in terms of restricted, repetitive, or stereotypical behaviors, interests and activities: (1) an abnormally intense or focused preoccupation with something or some activity; (2) inflexible adherence to rituals, including nonfunctional ones; (3) stereotypical and repetitive movements (e.g., hand or finger flapping); and (4) persistent preoccupation with parts of objects. PDD-NOS is the diagnostic label typically reserved for children who show similar, severe social and communication deficits as in autism, or who demonstrate stereotypic behaviors and limited interests, but who may not have exhibited the behaviors by age three or who do not formally meet all criteria in all categories.

Some clinicians view these developmental disorders along a continuum, with autism representing the most severe symptoms, PDD-NOS representing those next in severity, sometimes referred to as high-functioning autism, followed by Asperger's disorder. It is also important to note that other clinicians view the diagnosis of PDD with caution due to its broadly based DSM criteria (Buitelaar, Van der Gaag, Klin, & Volkmar, 1999). Still others argue that PDD tends to be given to older, rather than younger, children because the developing child with autism (a more severe disorder) who receives treatment often no longer meets the stringent diagnostic criteria after a few years. Additional concerns exist that labeling a child with "high functioning" versus "low functioning" autism causes one to customarily ignore a child's unique profile of strengths and weaknesses. Clinicians and parents might also be cautioned that if a child receives a diagnosis of PDD versus autism he may be excluded from services in some settings (e.g., school and certain state-funded programs).

Early in the first year of life, neurotypical (NT) children display emotions and appear to have significant interest in the emotional displays or states of others. Children as young as five to nine months will look at their caretaker's face to help guide their reactions to unfamiliar stimuli or situations (Striano & Berlin, 2005). In other words, they "check in" with a parent to help determine if they should be happy, scared, cautious, etc. In contrast, children suffering from autism fail to use such parental information as a guide in assessing a situation and or moderating their own emotional responses. They either do not realize that they can garner information about an unfamiliar situation from others' emotional displays or they simply cannot interpret these displays in the first place. Children with autism do not appear able to assume another person's perspective or viewpoint, either literally or figuratively, presenting severe social deficits. Recent neurological research suggests that the amygdala, a small structure in the brain's limbic system that aids in facial and emotional recognition as well as affective displays, may be impaired in children with autism (Klin, Jones, Schultz, Volkmar, & Cohen, 2002).

Neurotypical infants also demonstrate, by nine months on average, an interest in sharing emotional or social experiences with others. Children will often gaze or point at something in hopes of getting another's attention or to focus on a shared object. In contrast, children suffering from autism typically do not point at things or share one's attentional gaze, either for information or pleasure. If an autistic child wants a specific object, he may simply cry or tantrum, or grab a caretaker's hand and pull or lead her to the object. He uses the caretaker as a tool, a simple means, not realizing that he can gesture or cause another person to share the same perspective. There also appears to be little positive emotion in response to such activity among children on the spectrum. This lack of pointing, this inability to use nonverbal gestures in general to communicate, appears to be a hallmark and often striking symptom.

While many lay persons assume that children with autism are devoid of emotions, perhaps due to their typical, apparent disinterest in other children and adults, and often robot-like tone of voice, research suggests that autistic boys and girls do display a full range of emotions. Of course, one cannot always infer the inner experience of an individual from his outward appearance; however, it seems reasonable to assume that if someone is crying, he is experiencing some sort of distress or anxiety, if not more cognitively complex feelings such as disappointment or frustration. Sadly, quantitative research suggests that children with autism present more negative emotional displays, such as crying, sadness, fear and anxiety, than both typically developing children and those with mental retardation (Sigman & Capps, 1997). Although one cannot easily infer the internal experience of these children, one can probably assume that it is challenging or even overwhelming.

Many commonly observed characteristics or behaviors of children with autism are not articulated clearly in the DSM criteria, which read like a laundry list of problem behaviors. For example, "stereotyped and repetitive use of language or idiosyncratic language" includes readily identifiable, somewhat bizarre vocalizations called "scripting" or "echolalia." A child with autism will often repeat or echo everything he hears, in the absence of context or function. Take Shane, a three-year-old boy who hears his mother say, "Let's get our coats and hats on and go to the playground." Shane makes no movement to get his coat and shows no excitement about going outside. He simply states, "Let's get our coats and hats ... let's get our coats and hats." When watching *Sesame Street*, Shane will also echo the voices of Cookie Monster and Big Bird, droning "me want cookie" and "that makes me angry" in the absence of any appropriate social or emotional context.

During scripting, a child may repeat long passages of speech out of context and often in a monotone or, conversely, in exactly the same tone and volume as the speaker. Common passages are from favored videos or songs. For example, Chris, a four-year-old boy with autism, recites lines from Thomas the Tank Engine videos – without making a single mistake. He does not attempt to engage an adult or peer in order to interact with or listen to him while he speaks. While walking in a circle with his head down, he will recite an entire episode, which may take nearly twenty minutes. Many people assume that these children have exceptional memories (sometimes referred to as a splinter skill) because scripting can involve lengthy periods of time and thousands of words and phrases. Unfortunately, the same child may not be able to repeat four digits in succession or follow a one- or two-step instruction.

The absence of pretend play represents another hallmark feature of autism. By their first birthday, typical children engage in rudimentary imaginary play. For example, they may take a block and push it like a truck, or pick up a pretend phone and hold it to their ear. By 18 months, this play scheme is expanded to include multiple actions, such as using a comb to brush a doll's hair or offering a block to a Cookie Monster as a "cookie." The make-believe agents in these scenarios are passive recipients of actions or care. By two and a half years of age, however, NT children endow their imaginary playthings (dolls, action figures) with motives, feelings and goal-seeking behavior (see Sigman & Capps, 1997, for a review). In contrast, children with autism rarely, if ever, engage in spontaneous pretend play. When presented with a toy phone, a two-year-old with autism may, for example, repetitively bang the phone against a table, press one or two of the buttons over and over, or simply ignore it after a brief inspection. A typically developing child might pick up the phone and pretend to answer it, press it against the ear of another child or adult, or even offer the phone to a doll or puppet. Studies show that even children with mental retardation are more likely to engage in pretend or symbolic play than children with autism. Compared to NT children, boys and girls with autism are also more likely to wander about aimlessly than play with their toys, especially in the absence of some kind of guidance or structure (Kasari, Sigman, & Yirmiya, 1993).

Most children with autism display some form of repetitive, nonfunctional behavior or movements. These may include inappropriate play with toys, such as focusing exclusively on one part of a toy or using a toy in inappropriate ways. For example, a child may hold a truck upside down and spin the wheel over and over again. "Over and over again" may indicate *hours* spent in this activity if the child is not redirected, not merely minutes. A child might also take a toy telephone and repetitively drop it onto its cradle, over and over, missing the opportunity to play with the pretend phone as a functional object.

Many children with autism have motor skills and abilities to physically manipulate objects similar to those of their NT peers (Sigman, Ungerer, Mundy, & Sherman, 1986). The difference lies in the autistic child's apparent inability to engage those objects in ways that relate to social or functional representations. For example, some children do not "play" with their toys; instead, they line them up in rows or columns, over and over, for hours. And, disrupting this scheme in any way can cause significant distress to that child.

Nonfunctional, repetitive movements typically displayed by children with autism are referred to as "stim" behaviors or, while a child is performing them, as "stimming." A classic repetitive behavior is hand flapping, often with the arms down at the side or the arms extended. Other examples of stimming include toe walking (walking on one's toes for extended periods of time for no apparent reason), flicking fingers, head banging, walking in circles, and jumping repeatedly. Stimming may also represent an autistic child's attempt at self-regulation and stress relief. Many critics who argue that the significant increase in the number of children diagnosed with autism is due to expanded diagnostic criteria or general awareness in the population cannot dismiss the apparent neurobiological nature of these behaviors. A child in LA and a child in rural Minnesota are unlikely to "learn" such unusual and specific behaviors as hand flapping and toe walking from other children with behavioral problems.

Some studies suggest that as many as three out of four children suffering from autism are moderately to severely retarded (e.g., Cohen & Volkmar, 1997). However, it remains unclear to what extent low IQ scores are more a result of low intellectual functioning or a by-product of the test measures themselves. It likely is more important to view IQ scores in terms of their individual subtest scores and scatter. Performance IQ is almost always higher than verbal IQ among children suffering from autism, perhaps in part due to problems with measurement. Scattered scores are also more consistent with a picture of autism. A flat, low distribution of scores across all domains is more suggestive of retardation, or autism and retardation (Klin, Volkmar, Sparrow, Cicchetti, & Rourke, 1995). Because many children's IQ scores increase significantly with treatment (Lovaas, 1987), it remains unclear what proportion of children with autism actually are mentally retarded.

ADDITIONAL CLINICAL FEATURES

Neurotypical children in industrialized cultures, with a daily routine organized around eight-hour work days, tend to have a relatively well-established diurnal cycle. In other words, by one year, most parents of typically developing children are thankful that their infants no longer have their "nights and days" confused. In contrast, children with autism tend to have significant difficulty transitioning from periods of arousal to drowsiness and sleeping, which may serve as an additional warning sign for autism (James & Barry, 1980). Parents of children suffering from autism often indicate that their child's poor sleep cycle accounts for significant stress in their home.

Many children with autism fail to recognize signs of potential danger, and they may become seriously injured as they engage in dangerous physical activities (Sigman & Capps, 1997). Consider Timmy, who at age three began to climb trees in his family's back yard with remarkable speed and agility. This young boy was a fearless climber who would not respond to yells from his parents to come back down from branches that were ten to twelve feet above the ground. Constant surveillance was required to keep him from climbing the trees; this seemed to be his preferred activity whenever he was allowed outside. No amount of reasoning could convince him that this was dangerous. Timmy also climbed on top of furniture, including armoires, in the family home.

By eight months of age, NT infants possess visual acuity similar to that of adults. Even young infants will scan a human face, and by age one, children begin to examine the features of the middle of faces (Haith, 1990; Haith, Berman & Moore, 1977). But many children with autism tend to use peripheral vision to view objects, even when their vision tests as "normal." For example, Chad was a two-year-old who tended to spend hours turning his head sideways to look at corners and lines. He would often place his eyes so that they were level with the kitchen countertop and look down along the expanse of open countertop. He would also take a toy truck and look along the edge of the door rather than gaze or play with the truck itself. Other children with autism look at things with one eye at a time or may squint to look at people or things.

Because many typically developing children look out of the side of their eyes and use peripheral vision when afraid or upset (Tronick, Als, Adamsen, Wise, & Brazelton, 1978), one could infer that children with autism are so overwhelmed by internal or external stimulation that they revert to this form of more controlled and limited sensory input. However, making such inferences is not always appropriate because the internal experience of a neurotypical child and that of a child with autism may be completely different, and remains largely unknown (Sigman & Capps, 1997). When asked why he stared at lines, one four-year-old boy with autism replied, "I don't know. I just like the lines." Significantly more research is needed before we can understand this discrepancy.

Many children with autism demonstrate a strong preference for a dramatically limited diet. Some children will only consume foods that are one color, like orange or white, without exception. One girl diagnosed with PDD ate popcorn, white bread and baked potatoes, exclusively, for six months. When her parents forced her to eat something else, she would become so agitated that she would choke or vomit. No amount of praise or punishment would get her to deviate from her "white" diet. Other children will avoid foods with a certain texture, especially those that are crunchy. Still others will not eat foods that are sticky, such as peanut butter, because they do not want to feel the food on their hands or on the roof of their mouths. Even more unusual, children with autism will often smell inedible objects (e.g., pencils, books, dolls) or dramatically overemphasize their need to smell food before eating it. Unlike their NT peers who may exhibit some of these behaviors some of the time, these unusual behaviors are quite pronounced and severely limit the autistic child's caloric input or social interactions.

Additional sensory disturbances that children suffering from autism display include extreme auditory sensitivity and tactile defensiveness. After testing their hearing, and finding it within normal range, many parents report that their children with autism exhibit significant distress when exposed to certain sounds. For some unknown reason, mechanical sounds seem to cause the most distress. One mother reported that whenever she ran the vacuum cleaner, her four-year-old son would cover his ears, scream uncontrollably, hunker down on the floor or run upstairs, and even sometimes urinate on himself.

When asked what features of symptoms of autism are the most prominent, parents tend to include behaviors not identified as key diagnostic indicators in the DSM. Some of the more notable behaviors include severe tantrums that lead to serious injuries or last for hours, preventing families from going out in public; treating others as objects ("It's like I had no feelings; it was all about using me to get something"); and inappropriate affective displays ("Kaylee would laugh at imaginary things, I think. I had no idea what was going on in her head since she couldn't talk"). Still other parents with children who are verbal report, "I can't stand that robot-like voice. It's like the words are flat and he is dead inside." Still others mention an apparent lack of empathy: "I fell down and hit my knee really hard. I swore, and then the pain brought tears. And Joey just sat there and played with his cards, like nothing happened." Statements like this one explain why so many initial complaints to clinicians include, "I think my child is deaf or has a hearing loss."

EARLY WARNING SIGNS

Recent empirical findings suggest that many behavioral symptoms of autism can be detected within the first year of life, rather than in the third or fourth year (see Table 2.1). Despite the obvious value of early intervention (Tidmarsh & Volkman, 2003), particularly upon a child's developing brain, many clinicians remain unaware of these early warning signs, and children fail to receive crucial diagnoses and treatment. This is unfortunate because many studies suggest that parents begin to recognize changes or note serious concerns about their child's development around 12–14 months of age (e.g., Eaves & Ho, 2004). Consistent with the timing of the parental observations, the American Academy of Neurology now recommends that screening for autism (for all children, not simply those suspected of having autism) take place at one year of age (Filipek *et al.*, 2000). The Centers for Disease Control and Prevention (2005) have also embarked on a new awareness campaign, "Learn the Signs. Act Early." It thus becomes essential that practitioners take these edicts seriously and engage in informed patient screenings.

When a child is suspected of having autism, it often makes sense for clinicians to engage in a brief screening, and then, if warranted, follow up with a more comprehensive diagnostic series in order to form a definitive diagnosis. Screening is best if it includes information from parents, other caregivers and teachers, as well as an observation of the child in question. Basic questions about the mother's pregnancy, developmental milestones, social skills and language (or pre-language) skills are paramount. Furthermore, it is critical that practitioners become familiar with the emerging symptom presentation of autism among infants and toddlers.

The ability to make an early assessment becomes fundamental because the average age of formal diagnosis among children in the United States is currently four years. Even more striking, more than half of all children with autism are not diagnosed until after they enter the school system. In the UK, many children do not receive a diagnosis until they are six years old (Howlin & Moore, 1997). The reasons for this late age of diagnosis in both countries are unclear, but a lack of trained professionals (Smith, Chung, & Vostanis, 1994) and, until recently, a lack of brief, easy-to-administer screening instruments may underlie this problem. Fortunately, new instruments are available to help differentiate among other developmental delays and mental retardation at an early age (Goin & Myers, 2004). Many of these new screening tools now offer parents and clinicians the opportunity to identify at-risk or symptomatic children when they are toddlers or even infants.

Table 2.1 Empirically identified warning signs for autism

Age	Behavioral indicator
12 months	No social smile
	Lack of appropriate facial expressions
	Does not reach purposefully for objects
	Does not point to objects ("Where is the light?"; "Show me the light!")
	Does not respond or orient to name
	Ignores people
	Appears deaf
	Failure to produce pre-language sounds (babbling, cooing)
	Hand or finger flapping
	Hypotonia (low muscle tone or weakness; may include constant drooling)
18–24 months	Poor eye contact
	No display of joint attention (social gaze)
	Lack of pretend play
	Inability to imitate
	Lack of spontaneous social gestures (only waves "bye-bye" if prompted)
	Lack of interest in other children
	Failure to raise arms in anticipation of being picked up
	Aversion to social touch (may arch back to avoid contact with caregiver)
	Does not go to or seek out caregiver for comfort
	Does not speak single words or two-word phrases
	Inappropriate mouthing of objects
	Appears awkward or clumsy when rolling over, crawling, or sitting up
	Unusual postures, especially on the right side of the body
Any age	Loss of any language or social skills

Sources: Charman *et al.* (1998), Eaves and Ho (2004), Filipek *et al.* (2000), Lord *et al.* (2000), and Robins *et al.* (2001).

DIAGNOSTIC INSTRUMENTS

Various instruments require either trained observers, parental reports, or a combination of the two to evaluate a child's behavior. There are pros and cons in relation to parental versus clinical observations. Screening tools that rely on parental reports are subject to emotional biases, including denial, but early studies (Smith *et al.*, 1994; Vostanis *et al.*, 1998) suggest that the majority of parents who seek assistance regarding a possible diagnosis are unlikely to suppress information about their child's symptoms. Tests that require only parental reports also tend to be less expensive and easier to administer since they do not require a specific time commitment with a trained observer. However, marginally greater specificity appears to be obtained when clinicians are involved in administering at least part of the instrument themselves (Goin & Myers, 2004).

A number of commonly used tools for assessment are available. The Checklist for Autism in Toddlers (CHAT; Baron-Cohen, Allen & Gillberg, 1992) is a popular tool among clinicians and researchers. It comprises fourteen different items that include elements of parental and clinical observation. Five different domains: empathic response; spontaneous play; joint attention; goal detection; and imitation, are assessed. Empirical studies suggest that toddlers at 18 months, who subsequently received formal diagnoses of autism at later ages, manifested limited empathy, problems with social gazing during joint-attention tasks, inability to imitate and an overall lack of pretend play (Charman, Swettenham, Baron-Cohen, Cox, Baird, & Drew, 1998). The revised CHAT, or Modified Checklist for Autism in Toddlers (Robins, Fein, Barton, & Green, 2001), uses only parental reports but appears to identify toddlers who will develop autism.

The Childhood Autism Rating Scale (CARS; Schopler, Reichler, & Rochen-Renner, 1988) is a 15-item screening instrument designed to be completed by a trained observer or clinician. This scale is designed to be brief, and it can be used to assess children aged two or older. Like many of these scales, however, it is important to note that some state-supported agencies and other bodies are known to inappropriately give such screening instruments to parents to complete themselves. When completed by an untrained caregiver, it remains unclear to what extent the CARS, or any other of these instruments, remains reliable and valid. Each category on the CARS is scored on a Likert-type scale from 1 to 4, with higher numbers indicating more extreme or autistic-like behavior. For example, one item relates to the child's appropriate or inappropriate use of objects. Another relates to communication skills, and yet another relates to sensory input and integration. Although the CARS lacks specificity in terms of differentiating autism from PDD-NOS and other developmental disorders, it appears to be reliable in identifying children who suffer from autism. It also has a provision for differentiating between mild to moderate and moderate to severe forms of the disorder.

Another screening measure is the Social Communication Questionnaire (SCQ; Rutter, Bailey, & Lord, 2005), formerly known as the Autism

Screening Questionnaire (ASQ). The SCQ asks parents or caregivers to evaluate their child's behavior over a three-month period. It takes only ten minutes to complete and provides general cut-off scores that suggest whether or not a child should receive a more comprehensive, follow-up assessment. The primary drawback of the SCQ is that a child must be four years old before he can be evaluated with this instrument. Since new research suggests that children as young as 12 months can be identified as having moderate or severe autism, this is relatively problematic. Similarly, the Social Responsiveness Scale (SRS: Constantino *et al.*, 2003) is a relatively brief, 65-item rating scale that demonstrates reliability in identifying children who would benefit from a comprehensive clinical assessment for autism. Although it can be completed in approximately 15–20 minutes, it, too, is applicable only for children as young as four years old. Its primary positive feature is that it can be completed by a parent, caregiver, or teacher, and that it assesses not simply the presence or absence of symptomatic behaviors but their severity as well.

Other instruments require more time or training to administer. The Autism Diagnostic Interview-Revised (ADI-R; Lord, Rutter, & LeCouteur, 1994) has become an essential component of many research protocols that target childhood autism (Tidmarsh & Volkmar, 2003). The ADI-R is a comprehensive and lengthy interview, comprising nearly 100 questions administered to caregivers of children suspected of having autism. Approximately two hours are required to administer and code this test. This instrument can be used for children from two to eleven years old. Three primary areas of assessment include language and communication, social interactions and stereotypical behaviors and interests. One drawback of the ADI-R is that the caregiver must have intimate knowledge of the child's developmental history, including developmental milestones as well as current behavior. The ADI-R has demonstrated high levels of reliability, and it can be quite effective in differentiating autism from other developmental disorders.

The Autism Diagnostic Observation Schedule (ADOS) and the Autism Diagnostic Observation Schedule-Generic (ADOS-G; Lord *et al.*, 2000) have four different modules or versions that can be used with children as young as two through adolescence and adulthood. A trained clinician interacts and observes a child for approximately one hour and engages the child in a variety of activities, or "presses," designed to evaluate a number of abilities. The ADOS and ADOS-G can be used reliably with individuals who do not have language skills, as well as those who do. Examples of specific tasks being evaluated include response to name, joint attention, anticipation of social routine, responsiveness of social smile, and pretend play. Standard scores and cut-offs are available for diagnoses of PDD as well as autism. Although often used in research protocols and settings, clinicians can receive formal training in this instrument and use it in individual, comprehensive patient assessments.

The CHAT seems to be the screening instrument of choice for determining whether or not a child has autism, and whether or not her symptoms are significant enough to warrant a comprehensive assessment and subsequent, early intervention. The CARS has also received praise for its high levels of reliability and validity (Morgan, 1988), but the modified CHAT can be completed by parents or caregivers rather than professionals. When a thorough diagnostic assessment is required, the ADOS, or ADOS-G, is probably the better measure. Reporting specific scores on such diagnostic instruments also may become important when a child needs to meet or exceed certain criteria to qualify for a variety of school or community-based programs. In contrast, however, it is critical to note that clinical judgment has proven to be more accurate and stable (Cox, Klein, Charman, Baird, Baron-Cohen, Swettenham, Drew, & Wheelwright, 1999) in many instances than reliance upon any single diagnostic instrument, including the comprehensive ADI-R (Lord, 1995). In other words, an experienced practitioner can often provide concerned parents with an accurate diagnosis and afford those families the opportunity to engage in early intervention. It is probably best practice to use *both* clinical experience and empirically supported diagnostic tools to provide confirmatory evidence for a child's diagnosis, particularly if the child is an infant or toddler.

MAKING A COMPREHENSIVE DIAGNOSTIC ASSESSMENT

If a parent indicates significant concern about a child's development, or if a screening instrument suggests that a child is at risk for developing autism, a comprehensive diagnostic assessment becomes essential. The best assessment begins with a team of interdisciplinary specialists (Tidmarsh & Volkmar, 2003). A psychologist is often a critical component of such a team, as well as a language pathologist, developmental pediatrician, occupational therapist, audiologist, neurologist and physical therapist. In some situations, such as dealing with school districts or state agencies when applying for grant monies, the diagnosis may carry more weight if delivered by a psychiatrist or other MD. Both the child and the parents are interviewed and observed. Because approximately one third of children appear to regress, particularly in relation to language, social and play skills before their second year (Tuchman & Rapin, 1997), it is essential to gather information about the child's current and past behavior. Asking parents exactly when they became concerned about their child, and why, can provide valuable information.

Important topics to cover with parents include behavioral disturbances, sleeping habits, eating habits, accidents or other injuries, and the presence of developmental or neurological problems in other family members. For example, many children with autism have significant sleep problems (Schreck, Mulick, & Smith, 2004) and may sleep for precious few hours during the night. Some studies suggest that children with autism have higher resting heart rates and respiration levels than NT peers (James & Barry, 1980). Other children have apparent food allergies or sensitivities, or become so selective that they will only consume three or four food items. One three-year-old refused to eat anything but cold cereal, cheese crackers, and milk. (When asked why she could not get her child to eat a more varied diet, the boy's mother pulled up her shirt sleeve to reveal a series of deep scratches and bite marks.) Still other children appear to have suffered head injuries or concussions, which may account for some of their behavioral symptoms.

A visit to a well-informed developmental pediatrician is also strongly recommended. Various studies suggest that for a subset of boys with a head circumference significantly smaller than average at birth, a rapid increase in head circumference between 6 and 14 months may be a warning sign for autism (Courchesne, Carper, & Akshoomoff, 2003). If a child has severe diarrhea or constipation, or is significantly below his recommended weight, this must be taken seriously and testing for colitis, celiac disease, and gluten (the "sticky" or binding protein in wheat and flour products) enteropathy (Tidmarsh & Volkmar, 2003) becomes vital. Even though gastroenterological (GI) distress is not a specific diagnostic indicator, many children with autism present with significant GI distress, and the pain they experience daily is so severe that it may account for many of their tantrums and much of their inability to concentrate and learn.

CONDITIONS TO RULE OUT

Because so many children with autism appear deaf or unresponsive to their names, a visit with a child-friendly or pediatric audiologist can help rule out hearing loss. Painless electrical impedance tests can help parents and clinicians determine whether or not even infants have a properly functioning cochlea and auditory nerve. Using a soundproof booth and a series of flashing lights and interesting toys, expert audiologists can determine if even an infant hears novel sounds in her environment, and they can determine her auditory threshold with some degree of accuracy. This kind of testing also allows practitioners to determine whether the ear drum and bones of the middle ear are intact and functioning. Because many children with autism experience a high number of ear infections (McCandless, 2003), which can damage the inner ear and ear drum, this testing becomes prudent.

Other important disorders to rule out or treat concomitantly include Rett's syndrome, childhood disintegrative disorder, Fragile X syndrome, seizure disorders, tuberous sclerosis, and Landau-Kleffner syndrome. Rett's syndrome is seen almost exclusively in girls, with approximately one out of every 1,000 children affected. As the result of a chromosomal abnormality, little girls begin to display autistic-like behavior as young as six to 18 months of age. They may respond well to typical treatments for autism (e.g., behavioral and occupational therapies) and start to enjoy social interaction and develop some language skills. However, between two-and-a-half and five years of age the girls begin to decline and manifest easily identifiable, stereotypical hand-wringing or handwashing movements. Psychomotor skills in general, and trunk coordination specifically, decline until the little girl may have trouble running or walking. The diagnosis is determined through a blood test. The vast majority of children with Rett's syndrome also manifest severe seizures, further causing disruptions in learning and achievement. By five years of age, most of these children have difficulty walking and performing basic activities of daily living. However, there may be renewed interest in social interaction with others, especially with intervention. The majority of these children also suffer from moderate to severe mental retardation. (See Perry, 1991, for a review.)

Another chromosomal abnormality to assess for is Fragile X syndrome. A blood test can help determine whether or not a child has this disorder, which accounts for the largest number of retarded individuals, after Down's syndrome, in the United States. It is estimated that approximately five percent of children diagnosed with autism have Fragile X syndrome (Gilberg & Coleman, 1992). Children with both Fragile X and autism are found to have lower IQs and more severe behavioral symptoms than children with Fragile X alone. Among children with such a dual diagnosis, however, the level of Fragile X protein is unrelated to the presence or absence of autism, suggesting that an additional mechanism or environmental factor is taking place (Bailey, Hatton,

Mesibov, Ament, & Skinner, 2000). Intervention is similar to that of autism, including behavioral, speech and occupational therapy, although the outcomes are not firmly established.

It also becomes vital to rule out the presence of seizures among children suspected of having, or among those who have, autism. Studies suggest that by the time they reach adulthood, individuals diagnosed with autism have a one in three chance that they will experience at least two seizures (Volkmar & Nelson, 1990). The odds of seizure appear to peak in adolescence and decline with age. The presence of epileptic seizures has been linked to both mental retardation and gross motor problems. Similarly, some children diagnosed with autism may be suffering from Landau-Kleffner syndrome, also known as acquired epileptic aphasia. A sleep-deprived EEG is required to make this diagnosis, and once seizure activity is noted, anti-convulsant medication, steroids, or other hormones may be used to help prevent the occurrence of additional episodes.

It is also important to consider parents' responses to the results of diagnostic tests, especially ones used to rule out the presence of other disorders. One mother noted, "I cried after we found out Tyler's hearing was normal. Can you believe that? I actually wanted him to have some kind of hearing loss. I thought that at least then we could do something for him. Anything would have been better than the diagnosis of autism." Another father noted, "Yeah, I thought that if the EEG showed that Trevor had seizures, he could just go on medicine or something to take care of it. I didn't want to think that anything else could be wrong with his brain." Considering these kinds of responses, after a diagnosis is made, care must be taken to support the family as well as the child when providing recommendations for treatment.

COUNTERTRANSFERENCE AMONG CLINICIANS

Therapists face significant emotional challenges as they work with parents to determine if their child has a serious developmental disorder. Common experiences among therapists include denial, sadness, and anger, as well as feelings of confusion, when attempting to identify appropriate resources and tools for assessment. One therapist acknowledged that she delayed the appropriate diagnosis and treatment of one patient's child for approximately six months due to difficulties in processing her own countertransference. When asked what happened, she remarked that she had been seeing the child's mother in therapy for at least two years, and that her client suffered from moderate clinical depression with obsessive features. "It made sense that my patient would be overly concerned about her [infant] son's development. I mean, she was in elementary education, too, so I knew that she was probably obsessing about seeing her child in relation to all of the other 'problem' children she saw at work." This therapist also happened to specialize in treating children for ADHD and behavioral disturbances, so she felt as though she would know if something were really wrong. "I never met the child; I didn't think it was necessary. I mean, all kids get fascinated by lights and get fussy sometimes, or are a little slow to develop. I wasn't that worried about it, and I was trying to help this mom relax and enjoy the time with her baby." Four months later, when her child was approximately two years old, the patient and her family moved out of state. The therapist and patient continued a few sessions over the phone to aid in a difficult termination. During their last phone session, the mother admitted that she took her son to a developmental pediatrician and that he received a formal diagnosis of autism.

Two more years passed. Then the therapist received the news that her own four-year-old niece, who lived across the country, was recently diagnosed with autism. After a visit with her niece and her brother's family, the therapist could not believe how she had overlooked her own patient's concerns about her son. The therapist noted,

> I will never forget the feeling, sitting there [with my brother and niece] in that restaurant when I went to visit. I mean, I love kids. And here was Callie, sitting there with me, her mom, her dad, and all of these great toys and books around her, and we can't get her away from the window. She just sat there and stared at the lights in the parking lot. Sometimes she would smile at them or make this weird kind of screeching sound. But she had no interest in me. I could just feel the pain emanating from my brother. I felt sick to my stomach, that's how disconnected this child was. I had never experienced anything like it. It came to me as more of a feeling than anything else … So, I wish I could apologize. I lost contact with my ex-patient, and I know I shouldn't contact her now. But now I think I understand what it must mean to have a child with autism. And now I know much better when it comes to working with my own patients. It is definitely better to deal with that anxiety and fear directly, and be more aggressive than conservative when seeking expert advice and evaluation. But it also breaks your heart to have a patient, who is already dealing with so

much, get something else dumped on their plate. I just hope that my ex-patient can somehow forgive me. At least I hope that after hearing my story, [other clinicians] won't make the same mistakes that I did.

Consistent with this case example, additional evidence suggests that many clinicians fail to take parental concerns seriously and hesitate to give children a formal diagnosis (cf., Schall, 2000). Many healthcare providers seem to regard concerned parents as inappropriately alarmist, or worse, as annoying and difficult. Parents of children with autism often report that they knew "something was wrong," but that it took months or even years to convince a practitioner to form the appropriate diagnosis. For some practitioners, having to learn about new diagnostic testing and working through even more insurance paperwork can be frustrating as well. In light of such challenges, clinicians can be encouraged to obtain additional training through continuing education and peer supervision.

Because children with autism as young as 12–16 months, especially those with moderate to severe symptoms, can be diagnosed with a high degree of reliability, it becomes critical that concerned parents *never* be told, "Oh, your child will grow out of it" or some variant of "Einstein and many other famous people didn't talk until they were three, and they turned out to be just fine." Any time a parent, teacher or caregiver reports problems with a child's eye contact, lack of pretend play, inability to point to desired objects, little response to his name, disinterest in other children and toys, hand flapping or rocking under stress, or lack or loss of language or pre-language sounds, serious attention must be given to the possibility that the young child has autism or a related developmental disorder. Despite the challenges presented to both clinicians and parents, an appropriate diagnosis will allow a child to undergo early intervention, and derive as much benefit as possible from treatment.

Chapter 3

Autism: the experience for children, parents, and practitioners

> All I want is to hear his voice. If I could just know what was going on in his head. Why does he flap? Why does he stare at lines? Will he ever tell me he loves me?
>
> – Mother of four-year-old David, diagnosed with autism

Before undertaking any attempt to understand the basis for some children's autistic behavior or symptoms, one must acknowledge the vast array of behaviors exhibited by these children, and the distinct behavioral and temperamental differences observed among children on the spectrum. Parker is four years old. He is tall and overweight for his age. He tantrums frequently, speaks repetitively in a singsong voice, climbs on furniture and playground equipment without any fear, and tends to grab and break his toys as well as the toys of others. He also likes to run into people and knock them down. His parents refer to him as a "bulldog." Contrast this picture with Ricardo, who is also four years old. He, too, has been diagnosed with autism. Ricardo is average in height but significantly below average in weight. He tends to sit passively most of the time, staring out of the corners of his eyes. His primary stim is to flap his hands and toe walk. It is very difficult to get him to try to run or jump. He tantrums rarely and avoids physical contact with everyone. His therapist refers to him privately as "her little mouse."

Some children with autism are aggressive and bite, kick, or scratch, whereas others appear meek and passive, even when provoked. Some appear to be flurries of activity, always in motion, flailing, climbing, rocking, running, bouncing, or flapping, whereas other children seem like they move in slow motion, stare into space for hours, and hardly run or jump at all. Some are constantly seeking touch and may inappropriately accost strangers, while others recoil from even the gentlest touch.

Still other children appear pleasant and eager to please, while others seem to chafe under even the simplest of rules. In essence, although children may receive the same diagnosis of autism, there still appear to be basic differences in temperament and in symptom clusters.

Many children seem self-aware and recognize their behavioral differences, whereas other children appear unaware of their behavior, much less how it differs from others. For example, some children are nonverbal, but others are verbal and speak in full sentences. Some children learn to toilet, to eat with utensils, and to dress themselves. Others barely eat more than one type (or color) of finger food and wear diapers through childhood. Still other children play symbolically, or even have pretend or make-believe friends, whereas others sit and spin wheels on cars or trucks in a meaningless way. Yet other children suffering from autism require a rigid structure and routine, breaking into violent tantrums with any deviation, while others experience significant changes and do not appear phased. Some interventions are effective with some children, but others are not. Even physical differences are to be expected. Some children with autism are overweight; others appear gaunt. This may be related to differences in metabolism or the presence of food sensitivities or leaky gut syndrome (Edelson & Rimland, 2003). In essence, every child on the spectrum is different, which cannot always be readily explained. Thus, one cannot make simple attributions for any single child's behavior.

Some of the most significant insights to the experience of autistic behavior are provided by famous authors and playwrights who suffer from autism and who have subsequently achieved some degree of celebrity. These include Temple Grandin, prolific author and Ph.D in animal science; Tito Mukhopadhyay, a severely autistic adolescent boy from India who writes books and poetry but can barely speak; Donna Williams, an author who describes her childhood as riddled with anxiety and confusion; Luke Jackson, a teenager diagnosed with Asperger's syndrome; and Sue Rubin, a nonverbal woman who helped write and starred in the award-winning documentary about herself, *Autism Is a World*. Although Sue Rubin extols in a subsequent interview in *Newsweek*, "Tell everyone that nonverbal autistic people are intelligent!" (Kalb, 2005), parents and clinicians must consider that these powerful insights come primarily from adolescents and adults who may or may not represent the typical adolescent or adult with autism, or that they may not correctly or accurately identify their experiences as children. Many children currently suffering from autism, unfortunately, are unable to describe their own internal worlds. Yet, this type of insight, even if it is limited and anecdotal, remains invaluable. (Parents and clinicians alike may be interested in the books authored by these individuals. Please see the resource list for details.)

Many of these famous individuals have been able to find some way to communicate with the "outside world." Almost all were nonverbal as children and diagnosed as moderately or severely mentally retarded. Despite their children's lack of responsiveness (Sue Rubin's mother reported that she was like a "sack of potatoes" due to her unresponsiveness to touch and her extreme hypotonia; Kalb, 2005), most mothers were relentless in their pursuit of some kind of treatment, or at least continued to attempt to allow their children to interact with the environment in some meaningful or unencumbered way. Although this is important information, and it suggests that every attempt should be made to treat children with severe autism despite their apparent, behavioral indifference, care should be taken to insure that depressed parents do not feel that they are failures if their children do not respond, or if they begin to question the amount of time and resources that they spend on their child.

SELF-STIMULATORY BEHAVIOR

Some of the most common questions parents ask regarding their children with autism involve the rationale for self-stimulatory behavior or "stimming." For example, "Why does my daughter toe walk?," "Why does Peter flap?," "Why does John stare at lines?" For Tito Mukhopadhyay, who rocks and flaps at a frantic rate of speed while staring off into space, his jaw slack and mouth open, he describes having two separate "selves." One represents his inner sense of self as an individual, with thoughts, opinions, and concerns. His other self appears to represent his body and experiences a constant bombardment of sensory information. This bodily self appears to act independently of his thinking self. In his experience he can observe it, but he can control it no better than one can control the weather. Tito adds, "I know [my stimming] looks different … but I got into this habit to find and feel my own scattered self" (Shreeve, 2005, p. 22).

Donna Williams also describes considerable angst about establishing any sense of self, while functioning in the midst of heightened and distorted sensory perceptions. She recounts much of her childhood as being frozen or rendered helpless by "exposure anxiety," in which she experienced the world as excessive and overwhelming. Any attempt to establish a sense of self, as in "I" versus "we" or "you," or to even experience any form of self-awareness even by making a joyful facial expression or hearing the sound of her own voice, was experienced as psychically painful. Donna felt better "chattering away to myself, singing or making out sound patterns, in order to close out the impact of the invasiveness of others" (Williams, 2003, p.16). For her, stimming allowed her to maintain a boundary between self and other. Sadly, she also describes much of her internal experience as "bewildering [and] even terrifying" (p. 71).

For young children currently in the throes of autism, it is difficult to ascertain their inner dialogue or to make accurate attributions for such stimming. One four-year-old, Timmy, who used to flap wildly but stopped after two years of Applied Behavioral Analysis, Occupational Therapy, vitamin and mineral supplementation, and chelation therapy among others, suddenly started flapping again when he developed a yeast infection. When his mother saw him stimming, she panicked and yelled, "Timmy! Stop that!" Upon hearing this, Timmy stopped, turned to face his mother and said in what his mother described as a tone of hostility and finality, "No, I won't, and you can't make me." He then turned his back to her and began flapping. When his mother pleaded with him, "Please, Timmy, tell me why!", he turned to her and said icily, "Because I like it." After being treated with anti-fungal medication for a few days, Timmy stopped flapping. When asked about it subsequently, he would not reply or he would say that he "didn't know" why he did it.

Yet another child, John, aged six, began to flap after a series of stressful changes at home. When asked why he was flapping, he stopped and replied innocently, "What? ... I wasn't flapping." It thus remains unclear to what extent children have control over these stim behaviors, how much they are aware that they are even performing them, or to what extent they even realize that they are inappropriate. This is consistent with an adult on the spectrum who described swaying his head, banging it up against a shed, and jumping repetitively at recess until one of his teachers told him to stop doing it when he was 11. He recounts that it felt good, and that he simply did not understand why his teacher told him to stop (Anonymous, 2002).

Many adults with autism talk about limiting their stim behaviors to private places, such as their homes, or carefully selecting less noticeable stims like finger play instead of head swaying or rocking. However, a consistent explanation for stimming, whether it is flapping, jumping, rocking, or humming, is that it represents a way to self-soothe in the presence of stress or an overwhelming internal experience of sensory overload, or even as a way to combat boredom. When viewed akin to typical adults and adolescents who tap their feet, chew their pencils, twirl their hair, or crack their gum when bored or under stress, this makes a lot of sense. These examples, however, pose a stark contrast to children with severe autism who bang their heads repetitively, bite themselves, or pull out their hair in clumps. When asked why they engage in similar self-injurious behavior (e.g., cutting and burning), individuals suffering from borderline personality disorder or dissociative identity disorder express similar views that they are combating emotional distress, or that they need to reestablish some kind of body boundary in the face of sensory-based flashbacks. Based upon anecdotal evidence and the similarities between self-injurious behaviors in other forms of psychopathology, it is likely that stimming behavior, including that which is self-injurious, may represent the child's best or most familiar attempt at mastering his environment and modulating unbearable sensory overload or anxiety. Some stim behaviors, such as either seeking out or repelling touch (e.g., being squeezed like Temple Grandin, 1995), staring sideways or using peripheral vision to look at things, and head banging, may also have a basis in sensory processing or integration problems.

Despite how verbal or nonverbal a child is, professionals must consider that the child may hear or understand what is being said to him, even if it does not always appear that way. One 25-year-old college student diagnosed with autism noted with disdain, "Professionals were afraid to enter and explore my world, except perhaps to ... pathologize, and 'fix' my internal universe ... very few asked questions or asked ... why I behaved and expressed my feelings like I did" (Anonymous, 2002, p. 56). In essence, although many children with autism are accused of not having or demonstrating empathy, they themselves may be painfully aware that often little is shown to them by practitioners, who approach them only as a source of pathology, rather than trying to understand their reasons for exhibiting atypical behavior.

Other parents want to know why children obsessively line up toys or demand rigid schedules. Significant anxiety is often associated with transition or change for individuals suffering from autism. One young adult with autism suffered nightmares and anxiety attacks for three months before she was scheduled to move into a small apartment (Anonymous, 2002). Another 38-year-old man on the spectrum described living in a similar state of sensory overload, noting that things were manageable only when they stayed the same. He states, "If you were blind, I'm sure you would prefer things to stay the same [including the placement of the furniture]. I don't want the furniture ... [of my] social and learning environment ... moved in much the same way" (Anonymous, 2002, p. 35). In essence, rituals prevent undue stress and anxiety. No wonder this behavior is such a challenge to change in young children. While typical children inherently value any surprise, children with autism must often be taught to enjoy it, or at least to tolerate such uncertainty.

MENTAL RETARDATION, SPLINTER SKILLS AND SCATTERED SKILLS

An overview of many studies suggests that up to 75 percent of children with autism are mentally retarded (e.g., Rapin, 1997). However, studies also indicate that with intervention, many children gain significantly more points on IQ tests than those without intervention (Eaves & Ho, 2004). Because IQ tests purportedly measure general intelligence, which is supposed to be a static trait, it is unclear if treatment interventions cause an increase in actual intellectual ability, or whether they increase a child's ability to attend and communicate and thus perform better on such testing. Even though many nonverbal forms of intelligence testing are developed with the notion that they can gather reliable and valid information about a child's abilities, despite limited verbal skills, a child's level of motivation and interest can also influence the result of testing. Because many adults who were nonverbal as children describe "having things [language] come in" without being able to respond verbally at that point in time, one must consider that more children with autism are *not* mentally retarded than many studies suggest. EEG studies may also be of use to help determine if a child suffers from mental retardation. But, regardless of whether or not a child with autism has mental retardation, one simply cannot give up hope that interventions will work and make a significant difference.

Another factor that causes parents and teachers considerable angst regarding their children with autism is the expectation that their children have some kind of savant or special ability. The stereotype of Dustin Hoffman's character in *Rain Man*, who could count hundreds of dropped matches at a glance, memorize long series of numbers, and identify what day of the week a date falls on long into the future, persists for many lay persons today. However, studies suggest that fewer than 5 percent of all individuals with autism have such extreme splinter or savant-like skills (Obler & Fein, 1988). It is notable that many of these individuals who can multiply large numbers in their heads are quite limited in activities of daily living and basic communication. One theory about these limited, specialized and compartmentalized abilities is that they are "fast mapped" via the neural cortex and performed without conscious thought, concentration, or even volition. For parents, it sometimes is important to help them disregard such stereotypes or to avoid focusing exclusively upon their child's "special skill," if she does have one, in order to seek intervention in other areas of need.

What does appear more common, however, among children on the spectrum, is the finding that many intellectual functions appear "scattered." Many children can learn to read or draw well, for example, yet they cannot dress themselves appropriately for the weather or answer what appears to typical adults as a very simple question. The IQ subtests, including the subtests of both Verbal and Performance IQ, of many children with autism are not similar in value but often vary significantly. This apparent ability to excel in one area but demonstrate severe deficits in another does not appear logical, particularly to many parents and teachers. This scattered pattern of ability is similar to that often seen among children suffering from ADHD; parents can become easily frustrated and state things like, "How can this child concentrate on video games for four hours at a stretch and then be unable to hold a conversation for five minutes with me?" These differences in skills and abilities can appear as a function of sensory or information processing as well.

Dawn Prince-Hughes, a professional writer and anthropologist with autism at Western Washington University, notes that the apparently disjointed writing provided by adults diagnosed with autism simply reflects a different type of information processing, and that it actually indicates "divergent possibilities … at a staggeringly fast pace" (2002, p. xii). In children, this type of disjointed thinking may represent tangential thinking, in which a child's attentional or executive skills are so impaired that by the time they finish hearing the end of a question, they have already forgotten the first half of it, or they begin to think of something else related to what the person was asking them about. In essence, many children on the spectrum have significant difficulty with auditory processing and simple semantics.

For example, a therapist asked John, a six-year-old with autism who scored 89 via IQ testing and is not mentally retarded, "What season is it? How does the weather look like outside today?" John looked around, said, "Oh," while he turned to the window, paused, and then said proudly to his therapist, "Yes, I see the sun outside. This is a big window. You have a little window in your office!" When she responded, "Yes, John, I do. But, I asked you what season it is," he looked confused, as if this was the first time he heard the question. John responded again, "Winter is a season, and summer is a season, too!" When presented with four pictures that represent the four seasons, and asked the season again, John touched the card with the appropriate season, spring, and said, "Yes, this is it! It's spring today." Clearly he knew the answer but had difficulty retrieving and conveying the information. This type of communication, in which a child often appears to have mastered basic vocabulary and concepts but cannot always answer a simple question, often bolsters assumptions that most children with autism are mentally retarded. It is often critical that parents and teachers understand that many children with autism are not "retarded, slow, or dumb" (therapists must be prepared for parents or teachers to use such words to describe or ask about their students), but they process information differently. Care also must be taken to prevent children themselves from feeling grossly inadequate. Helping them use their more functional skills and types of processing to regulate their own internal states and navigate often confusing social environments remains crucial.

SENSE OF SELF AND OTHER

Adults with autism often remark about how their social sense is very different from that of others. For some who describe their early childhood, when their symptoms were most severe, being "social" was not even a working concept. For example, Donna Williams describes herself as a child by stating, "I was ... social with the dirt, the trees, the grass ... the rolls of carpet at the hardware store, the books of wallpaper samples ... and the smell and lickable surface of patent leather" (2003, p. 16). Other adults describe, even in their current lives, that interacting in social settings, with its requisite perspective taking, is exhausting or even irritating and unnecessary. Some adults describe learning or adopting "social modules," such as always smiling during gaps in conversation or saying "thank you" whenever they are at a loss for what to say (Anonymous, 2002). Luke Jackson extols the value of being very polite (2002). Still others on the spectrum describe feeling that they are aliens from another planet, trying to learn social norms and cues. Temple Grandin certainly echoes those thoughts in the essay Oliver Sacks wrote about her in *An Anthropologist on Mars* (1995). Many individuals with autism report that they can engage in social interaction, but at a significant drain of mental resources and psychic energy; it rarely becomes an automatic task.

Sadly, most adults with autism who discuss experiences from their childhood, who may represent only a specialized subsample of individuals with autism, describe living a life generally filled with anxiety and confusion. This description of one's internal experience on the spectrum is consistent with previous research showing that children with autism typically display more negative emotions than both typical children and children with mental retardation (Sigman & Capps, 1997). Awareness of this overwhelming tendency toward anxiety and fear among children suffering from autism may help practitioners maintain appropriate levels of empathy, particularly when working with a client's challenging behavior.

WORKING WITHIN THE FAMILY SYSTEM

The most effective treatment for children suffering from autism appears intensive, requiring many hours a day across many settings (Erba, 2000). Clinicians must engage parents, and work with the family as a system in order to gain the best treatment compliance and to bolster treatment effectiveness. In other words, therapists must treat the entire family and not just the "identified patient" or child. While this seems reasonable given common sense, a recent empirical study found that one of the best predictors of how a child responds to treatment, regardless of the type of treatment, is how the mother is faring psychologically. Of all other family members, mothers of children with autism appear to present with the most psychiatric symptoms, and estimates suggest that between one- and two-thirds meet criteria for clinical depression (Bitsika & Sharpley, 2004; DeMyer, 1979). Mothers and fathers of children suffering from autism are more likely to feel less confident in their parenting and to experience greater marital distress than parents of typical or mentally retarded children (Fisman, Wolf, & Noh, 1989; Rodrique, Morgan, & Geffken, 1990). So from the beginning, the mental health of parents must be considered in any treatment plan, and the psychological needs of parents must be addressed immediately, particularly at the time of diagnosis.

When providing parents with a diagnosis of autism for their child and information about possible interventions, clinicians must also consider whether the parent or parents have adequate social support. For example, do they have enough instrumental support (e.g., financial assistance, knowledge about insurance coverage, respite care) and emotional support (e.g., supportive friends, church group). Therapists should insure that parents leave such a difficult session with clear options for therapy for themselves and for support groups in their community (the ASA and NAS have many local chapters), or internet options if they live in an isolated area. Some parents may be unaware of government-sponsored programs such as Medical Assistance, which is available in some states, and the Family Medical Leave Act. The needs of single mothers and blended families must also be addressed.

The strain upon parents is significant. The incidence of depression among parents of children with autism appears greater than among parents of children with terminal cancers (Hughes & Lieberman, 1990). Many parents, including step-parents as well as grandparents and other guardians, commonly experience post-traumatic stress disorder, depression, anxiety, marital problems, and substance abuse at various stages in their child's diagnosis and treatment. Due to such stressors, the divorce rate for parents of children with autism is thought to be much higher than the national average of approximately 50 percent.

Just as it is critical to consider the internal experience of a child with autism, practitioners must understand the experience of parents as well. Jane, mother of Peter, describes the day when she received official notification from a development psychologist that her child had autism:

> I remember that I really wanted this diagnosis. I knew something was wrong with Peter for a long time, and that no one wanted to listen to me. But when I heard the words out of [her] mouth, that's when it really hit me. It was the day before my son's third birthday. It was the worst day of my life. We drove home, and I remember putting the paper [with the official diagnosis] on the kitchen table, preparing to call the state office to get medical assistance. Then I had to turn to try to distract Peter who was spinning in circles and keening at the top of his voice. [Peter was nonverbal, would not make eye contact, and did not play with any toys.] After I got him to stop for a minute, I felt like I was watching myself outside of my body. I slumped to the floor, put my head down on the kitchen floor, and began to cry. I mean, really cry, like sob, like I thought I would cry and never stop. I had those huge sobs when your whole body shakes and your chest hurts. I thought that his life was over and that mine was, too. I wanted to know what happened to the little boy I always wanted. I wanted to know how I could have gone wrong as a mother. I wanted to know why I just couldn't go to Home Depot with my kid to do some shopping. I was scared out of my mind. I wanted to know why

my kid wouldn't say anything, much less "I love you." And after about 25 minutes of sitting there sobbing, I realized that Peter didn't even acknowledge my presence or what I was doing. It was as though I didn't even exist, and that he was some weird kind of robot that didn't notice or care about anything because his mind was all broken. Then I cried some more. It was the worst day of my life.

With intensive treatment, Peter is now six years old, verbal, and doing fairly well in kindergarten with the help of an aide.

Still other parents fight the possibility of any diagnosis. One mother of a five-year-old boy, Paul, kept "shopping" for a psychologist who would label her child with a nonverbal learning disability or Asperger's syndrome instead of autism. Paul would begin to make progress in occupational therapy or a social skills group, when suddenly his mother would pull him from that clinic. A pattern emerged in which Paul's mother was approached by professionals who confronted her about her child's behavior, and the benefits of more intensive services, and she simply could not tolerate this narcissistic injury. She even ostracized parents of other children with autism at local support groups because she kept insisting that her child "wasn't so bad [like yours.]" One mother from such a support group remarked, "Yeah. I got sick of [the mother] acting like her kid was better than mine. Her kid would sit there and suck his thumb while rocking, for god's sake. He doesn't even talk and she's calling him Asperger's." (Coping with heightened emotions and real or imagined competition among other parents, including those in support groups, can add to some parents' anxiety, as well.) After about a year in which various professionals in the local community tried to help Paul, his mother ended up relocating the family in order to find a school that specialized in nonverbal disabilities. Unfortunately, Paul suffered setbacks each time because transitions were particularly problematic for him.

Some suppositions about why parents of children with autism are more depressed than parents of children dying of cancer include parents of children with autism facing uncertainty about their child's condition, limited social support for the disorder, particularly when a child has a tantrum in public, and little or no insurance coverage. One clinically depressed mother of a five-year-old with autism noted,

I mean, if I just knew that Brett was retarded or had some kind of weird genetic disease, and I knew he would never get better, that would almost be easier. I'd know exactly what to expect. It would totally suck, but I could plan on what he would need in case I wouldn't be around, and I'd know how to spend my money and for what treatments. Right now, I don't know if Brett is really going to get better or not. Do I spend all of my money now on ABA and private schools? At the rate I'm going, for over $8,000 a year after insurance and including tuition, I don't think I'm going to have much [money] left by the time he's a teenager. What if this stuff doesn't work and he needs private school more then?

Not being able to go out easily in public, due to severe or frequent tantrums, is another basis for such depression (Dunn, Burbine, Bowers, & Tantleff-Dunn, 2001). One mother of a four-year-old with autism remarked,

> Yeah. Going anywhere is such a pain in the ass. So my kid yells and screams, and he looks too big for his stroller. If the fluorescent lights make a buzzing sound he is going to freak. If he sees a clown or some kind of weird advertising thing, he is going to freak. Maybe he shits his pants [Mike is not yet potty trained] and people smell it before I can get to the bathroom. You wouldn't believe the way people look at you and the things people say ... I just love the fucking bitches who whisper way too loud, you know, so that you can hear everything and they say things like, "any parent can control their child if they just use discipline," and "my kid never acted like that" and shit like that. Or someone comes over to talk to your kid and they get really freaked out when they just start flapping and making weird sounds. Welcome to my world. You know what, I'm sick of being barricaded in my house. I deserve to go out, too, but I can't get a sitter. Could you?

When an insightful father of a child with autism was asked to consider the difference between perceptions of children on the spectrum with those of children suffering from other ailments, he responded, "Sure it's different. Some kid, god forbid, with cancer, walks around with a bald head and a baseball cap, I feel bad even saying this, but everyone is going to feel sorry for that kid and their parents. With my kid, everyone looks at him and me like we're assholes. They just see his behavior and they don't get it. It's not like our kids walk around with crutches or a cast on their leg. People just assume the worst, and then treat us and the kids that way. It's kind of like a vicious cycle."

Because it often seems easier to talk to patients about sex than money, practitioners must be encouraged to discuss difficult financial matters with their patients and their families. Many families with children who suffer from autism face difficult financial decisions and stressors. One therapist described a patient's anger and frustration as he pondered, "Should we go on a trip to Disney World with all three kids, or do we skip it and use the extra money to get George better treatment? I'm OK with the fact that I will never be a millionaire or anything like that, but how am I supposed to make these kinds of decisions? I hate feeling like I have to pick and choose between my own kids." Another mother of a child with autism had to make the choice about whether to get a second mortgage on her house to keep her son's participation in ABA and to keep him enrolled in a good private school. There is no right answer to managing one's money, but therapists can help parents communicate openly about how they plan to allot valuable resources (Hillman, 2006).

Just as many therapists are taught that it is important to be a "good enough," rather than perfect, therapist, many parents can be helped to recognize that they, too, can be a "good enough" parent (cf., Winnicott, 1951). Guilt is a common feeling among mothers and fathers of children with autism. One mother noted, "I hate it that I get upset when I think about spending the weekend together, especially if one of my son's therapists is on vacation. I mean, I have to think about filling up the day, about how I can't just jump in the car and go places, about how I'm not going to do anything fun. It's just terrible. It's like I can't look forward to being with him. I long for him to go off to school, even though it's only a few hours a day. Aren't I the worst mom in the world?" Parents in this case must be taught to recognize that thoughts and actions are separate, and that one does not have to like or enjoy being with her child all of the time, particularly when he engages in inappropriate behavior.

Therapists can also help parents acknowledge that feelings of anger and guilt are normal and probably to be expected in such a situation. Another mother articulated, "Sometimes I feel like I can't believe this is happening to me. I mean, I do everything I can. I quit my job to stay home with Aaron. I spend over 700 dollars a month on treatments since insurance won't cover it. But I still feel like 'I've got nothing.' My kid won't even look at me or hug me. He is no way normal and I'm really pissed off. Of course, when I go to bed crying, I guess I'm sad."

Based on general principles of operant conditioning, practitioners must understand that, when dealing with an unresponsive or combatant child, it takes parents a tremendous amount of energy to continue in their pursuits of both love and treatment. Some parents describe years in which they received no speech, eye contact, or physical contact with a child. It also is critical to avoid falling into the trap of telling such parents, "Well, what you are experiencing is normal for any parent," because, in most instances, it is not. Clinicians can recognize the parent's expanding roles as parent, teacher, advocate, nurse, occupational therapist, disciplinarian, financial advisor, caregiver, and researcher. Therapists can also provide essential guidance in time management, anger management, and the ability to tolerate ambiguity.

Another critical issue often ignored in work with parents is that of loss and grief. Parents have hopes and aspirations that their child will do well in the world, have friends, enjoy school, adopt a trade or career, and marry and have children of their own. For parents of children with autism, this dream is often replaced with fears and nightmares. One mother stated, "Oh, my god. Who is going to take care of Ryan if something happens to me? Are we going to have enough money to take care of him as he gets older? I mean, I can't even let myself think too long about whether or not he'll ever have a date for the prom or have his first job. I just can't take it right now."

Especially in the early stages of diagnosis and treatment, parents must be given permission to grieve and acknowledge the loss of the child they imagined having. Sometimes with help, parents are able to reflect upon this incident and make new attributions. For example, one father stated, "You know, as a psychologist, I always valued talking and communicating as my number one priority. This [autism] is a cruel irony. My son can't even speak more than a few words right now. But, when he does say one of his words, or if he does hug me, I don't take it for granted. I see so many parents telling their kids to quiet down or shut up, or hurry them off to school, and I don't think I will ever be like that. Every little thing Brent does is like a little diamond I find in the dirt. And I won't give up on him. I need to keep holding on to high expectations." Regardless, one cannot ignore the practical concerns that responsible parents must have regarding their child's care.

One widely adopted program that helps parents take a primary role in their child's treatment is the Treatment and Education of Autistic and related Communication Handicapped Children (TEACCH) program (Schopler & Olley, 1982). Although some criticism of the program has been made because it typically places fewer demands upon a child to adapt and perform in typical settings, what it certainly does well is emphasize the role and education of parents (Hamilton, 2000). Essential elements include parental therapy and one-on-one parental training. If one parent is less inclined to seek psychological counseling than another, this TEACCH program may make therapy seem more palatable or less threatening because it is simply a standard part of a program designed for their child. In essence, parents do not have to admit having a problem or present a desire to address their own depressive symptoms; it is done automatically for them as a programmatic requirement.

When working with parents of children with autism, couples therapy could be instituted as a prophylactic measure as well. Parents and therapists should be aware of some common dynamics that can develop during the course of a child's treatment. For example, if one parent quits a job to stay home full time with the child, that parent, typically the mother, may become the primary caretaker and therapist. Sometimes the other parent, typically the father, becomes ostracized, minimized, or discouraged from interacting with his child or taking an active role during treatment. One father noted, "I got sick of Joan saying, 'Well, we're doing it THIS way! I've been the one taking him all over god's green earth while you've been at work, so I don't have time to explain this or that to you all the time.'" Practitioners must help these parents to develop some role assignments yet maintain flexibility and open communication between them. (It is sometimes easier for one parent to be the point-person for a physician, for example.) Parents at work must also make efforts to provide relief or respite care for the primary caregiver, keeping in mind that social isolation is one of the better predictors of parental depression.

The use of drugs and alcohol as escape mechanisms, as well as hoping inappropriately for miracles, is associated with lower marital satisfaction among families living with autism. Helping parents to take some time for themselves and to interact with other people about things unrelated to autism appears related to better coping. Other coping styles associated with more positive outcomes include fighting for what is appropriate (e.g., insurance payments; more hours of intervention from a school), expressing anger about situations appropriately, seeking social support, finding faith in organized religion or spirituality, and prioritizing what is most important in life (Dunn *et al.*, 2001). Practitioners should also be aware that grandparents may be an untapped source of emotional and instrumental support.

Although limited research is available regarding the extended family of children with autism, some insight can be gleaned from work regarding siblings of children with autism. Siblings often receive less time and fewer resources from parents than the identified child. Sometimes this is difficult to avoid. For example, one child may require speech therapy and occupational therapy twice a week, at a cost of $300, or more, per month. However, it is best to help parents communicate openly with their typical children about their sibling's needs and the division of time and resources, at an age-appropriate level. Attempts should be made to spend special time or engage in special activities with typical children. In other words, no one can parent equally all of the time, but parents can do their best, and often small efforts (e.g., taking the typical child out alone to dinner or to play at the park for half an hour) have a significant impact (e.g., Hastings, 2003). It also can be beneficial for both typical and autistic siblings to engage in therapeutic activities together. Fortunately, empirical studies suggest that siblings of children suffering from autism are generally free from other diagnosable psychological disorders (Pilowsky, Yirmiva, Doppelt, Gross-Tsur, & Shalev, 2004).

Common patterns for therapists to look for in families of children with special needs include unrealistic expectations of excellence for typical children, to somehow "make up" for their special-needs sibling, and anger toward the typical child for not being understanding enough or flexible enough about her sibling's needs. It is common for older, typical siblings to be embarrassed about their brother or sister's tantrums or unusual forms of communication. Parents can learn to empathize with their typical child's feelings and help them to engage in appropriate behavior. Sometimes there are also benefits. One typical sibling of a younger brother with autism noted, "Sometimes it really bugs me how he breaks some of my things, but he's pretty cool ... He has to work extra hard to do things. I don't know if I could work as hard as he does. And, now, I make sure that no one picks on him, cause I wouldn't like it, either."

Practitioners should be aware of the challenges inherent in working with children with autism. Insurance coverage may be limited, and an intensive, integrative approach is required for effective intervention. Work with a mute, physically aggressive child may require a specific behavioral approach, whereas work with a child's depressed parent may be best suited for insight-oriented therapy. And, therapeutic intervention with a family, including parents and neurotypical siblings, may call for yet another, different, systems approach. Clinicians must become comfortable with shifting back and forth between advocacy, primary care, and eclectic forms of therapy. Knowledge of current, empirically based research is required, as well as an ability to work well with other healthcare professionals. The overarching goal is to treat the entire family, not merely the identified patient.

Chapter 4

Applied behavioral analysis: the gold standard and beyond

> I credit ABA with saving my son's life. I know it.
>   – Michelle, mother of a five-year-old son with autism

In their formal practice guidelines for the treatment of childhood autism, the Surgeon General's Office of the United States currently calls for 30–40 hours per week of one-on-one, behaviorally based treatment. The specific form of recommended therapy is known as Applied Behavioral Analysis (ABA). The basis for this treatment is the use of discrete trial training (DTT) or learning (DTL) in which a therapist and child work on various skills and behaviors. Although it has different names, the first training programs developed are now referred to as Lovaas-based ABA. Newer, modified programs may be referred to as simply ABA, Applied Behavior Analysis for Verbal Behavior Model (ABA/VB or VB), National Environment Training ABA (NET ABA), or modified ABA. For simplicity, ABA will be used here generically, and its specific form will be clarified (e.g., Lovaas training or simply Lovaas) when necessary. The critical, common denominator for all forms of ABA is the desire to increase the types and frequencies of appropriate behavior through positive reinforcement.

ABA is often credited with significantly changing a child's behavior and fostering the development of critical life skills. Positive behaviors targeted in ABA-based programs include initiating speech, using the bathroom, and attending to parents and teachers. ABA can also be used to help reduce the frequency and intensity of self-injurious and self-stimulatory behaviors. Both the short- and long-term effectiveness of ABA have been reported by Ivar Lovaas (Lovaas, 1987; McEachin, Smith, & Lovaas, 1993), and other researchers (Anderson & Romanczyk, 1999; Smith, 1999), although some experts caution that not all children respond equally to such programs (Shea, 2004; Sherer & Schreibman, 2005). Despite some controversy over the specific preferred type of intensive behavioral intervention or ABA, virtually all researchers concur that a traditional, psychodynamic approach alone is ineffective against autism (National Institute of Health, 1975).

Many parents speak about ABA with awe and wonder. One mother of a four-year-old son with autism noted, "Dallas never talked before. He was three years old and never said a word. I prayed for him to talk, I begged him to talk. It was like he was in his own world and I could never reach him … But after we started working with that desk and chair, and after the screaming and fighting stopped, Dallas started looking at people, and he started looking at me. Then it was 'cookie' and 'car' and then … 'Mommy.' I will never forget that day, as long as I live, when he looked up at me from his little chair and said, 'Mommy.'" Another benefit of such intensive behavioral treatment, one not often discussed in the literature, is the likely ability to provide additional structure and support to families (Lovaas, Smith, & McEachin, 1989) during the midst of a highly ambiguous and overwhelming situation.

THE HISTORY OF ABA: IVAR LOVAAS

Ivar Lovaas is considered the founder of ABA-type interventions, and his specific treatment approach is commonly referred to as Lovaas training or simply "Lovaas." He conducted the bulk of his work at UCLA. His seminal work was published in 1987 in the *Journal of Clinical and Consulting Psychology*, in which he reported that 47 percent of the children suffering from autism in his treatment condition "achieved normal intellectual and educational functioning, with normal-range IQ scores and successful first grade performance in public schools" (Lovaas, 1987, p. 3). The children in his study received more than 40 hours per week of intensive, one-on-one behavioral intervention for at least two years. Parents were also trained to deliver treatment, so that learning "could take place for almost all of the subjects' waking hours, 365 days a year" (p. 5). For Lovaas, it was critical that treatment be intensive (i.e., one-on-one), that it occur both at home and at school, and for long periods of time. Lovaas reasoned that typical children learn through observation and imitation practically all of their waking hours, whether they are in a formal school setting, playing with their toys, or interacting with parent or peers at home (Lovaas *et al.*, 1989). For children with autism, who often spend significant periods of time involved in self-stimulatory behavior, with limited or no interest in interacting with others, such opportunities for typical learning are significantly curtailed.

Most children start Lovaas programs in a specialized therapy room in the home (or clinic). These rooms contain small tables and chairs and limited wall decorations to minimize distraction. Because sitting at a table quietly engaged in some task proscribed by an unfamiliar therapist does not represent typical behavior for a child with severe autism, sometimes weeks are needed until a child will readily sit at a table prepared to attend. Some specialists recommend that the child be asked to sit in the chair (or led to the chair) and reinforced for sitting even if it is only for a few seconds. Shaping occurs when the child is required to sit for longer and longer periods of time to receive his reward. Documentation is also critically important. All discrete trial learning programs are identified and chronicled by both parents and therapists. Flashcards are often used to guide trials. For example, a child may be asked to sit and attend while a therapist shows a series of pictures. For each picture, the child would be asked to identify the picture (e.g., cookie) and receive praise (or food or some other reinforcer) when he completes the task, or completes the task within a certain time limit or with a certain percentage correct.

Lovaas' behavioral intervention is based upon the Skinnerian principles of operant learning that all college students learn in their introductory Psychology courses. When a child's behavior is reinforced, it will increase in frequency. When a behavior is ignored or when a privilege is removed in response, the behavior will diminish in frequency. Before extinction occurs, however, the child is likely to show a burst of increased inappropriate or nonpreferred behavior. Current Lovaas-based programs proscribe only positive reinforcement or the ignoring of negative behavior; physical punishment is not employed or endorsed (see Lovaas *et al.*, 1989). The goal is for positive behaviors (e.g., attending, sitting still and listening to a teacher, following simple directions) to generalize across settings, and to fade necessary prompts. In other words, a child will eventually engage in appropriate behavior at home, at school, and in a novel setting without specific directions or overt cues.

Another critical factor is that any well-run ABA program is tailored specifically to each individual child. A "one-size-fits-all" or generic approach is not effective, and parents should be cautioned to avoid clinicians or agencies that promise such a generalist approach (Hillman, 2006). Developing an individualized program typically requires that the clinician spend a number of hours with the child and his parents to observe the child in various settings, assess the child (often employing a standardized measure or guide such as the Assessment of Basic

Language and Learning Skills or ABLLS; Partington & Sundberg, 1998) and receive critical feedback from parents and teachers about areas of strength, weakness, and concern.

FUNCTIONAL ANALYSIS

Additional, functional analyses (i.e., an objective analysis of the child and her environment) are critical assessments conducted by a clinician to determine what function or purpose any specific behavior serves. For example, a child with autism (or any child) may tantrum for a variety of reasons. Helping a child to significantly reduce tantrums and pay attention to another person (e.g., paraprofessional, parent, teacher) provides a basis of good behavior consistent with learning. Without such basic attentional skills as a foundation, the development of language or advanced play skills is unlikely. In essence, reducing the frequency and severity of tantrums and increasing the frequency of behaviors that encourage attention to others should be the initial goal of any intervention program. Attentional skills are requisite in order to provide the best learning environment for the child.

Knowing what function a behavior serves, such as a tantrum, will allow a clinician to identify the best way to reduce that problem behavior. In terms of tantrums (or any specific activity), a child's behavior serves four primary functions: communication, escape, self-stimulation or attention. For example, a four-year-old, nonverbal child, Andy, tantrums because he is hungry for some more hamburger, is unable to communicate his needs to his father, and becomes frustrated. Tantrumming is his only way to communicate. At some point later in the same day, Andy may tantrum because he no longer wants to sit at the dinner table. He tantrums as an attempt to escape a situation. A few minutes later, Andy may tantrum and bang his head on the table, this time as a way to engage in self-stimulatory behavior (i.e., stim), much as many well-adjusted adults tap their pencils, twirl their hair, tap their feet, watch TV absent-mindedly, or daydream as a self-soothing activity when bored or anxious. In yet another example, Andy may tantrum because he wants attention from his mother, who is busy writing a business plan on her computer.

Understanding the function of a behavior is essential in order to select the appropriate plan to reduce its frequency and intensity. Choosing the wrong intervention may actually increase the frequency of the inappropriate behavior. If a parent or teacher ignores the tantrum, the child may no longer tantrum, but another behavior, which may be even more adverse (e.g., biting or self-injurious behavior), will take its place as a further attempt to communicate. If the behavior is an attempt to escape, one possible solution is to ignore the tantrum, help the child to enjoy the activity by using positive reinforcers, or teach the child to communicate "all done." In Andy's case, his parents learned to give him a small piece of candy for every three minutes that he sat with them at the dinner table. He was also taught the sign for "down." After fifteen minutes, Andy was allowed to motion "down" and leave the table. His tantrums diminished almost immediately. With self-stimulatory behavior, however, it is critical to note that if one attempts to extinguish the behavior, some other, potentially even more inappropriate, form of stimming will takes its place. For example, one child who was prevented from spinning the wheels on his favorite truck began to stare blankly at lines and shadows. In keeping with Andy's situation, when Andy's aunt prevented him physically from rocking wildly during a tantrum, Andy began to scream at the top of his lungs and gouge at his eyes instead. This stim behavior became more ingrained and frequent, even when his aunt was not present.

As noted by one seasoned clinician, stim behaviors cannot be stopped, but only altered or redirected (E. Fisher, personal communication, July 18, 2005). One way to approach this is to distract the child with a desired activity. Another is to help the child modify his stim so that it is less noticeable or blatantly inappropriate to others. For example, one child who flapped his arms wildly was taught to "wipe his hands" along his shirt when excited. This behavior allowed the child to soothe himself and appeared much more "normal" and unobtrusive to others around him. When he learned some language, this little boy was taught to say, "So cool!" or "Check it out" when he was very excited. His peers were much more likely to approach him to play. Because Andy's clinician and occupational therapist (OT) determined that Andy probably banged his head to receive rhythmic, deep pressure in an attempt to soothe himself, he was redirected to use a weighted vest and trampoline during tantrums. After many months of intensive work, Andy was further redirected to use a small squeeze or stress ball. He still "stimmed," but in a way that was not going to cause him serious injury or prevent him from interacting well with others. He could take the little ball along in the car and was even permitted to bring it to school in his pocket.

If a behavior's function is to gain attention, ignoring the behavior can be quite effective. Teaching the child other, more positive ways to get attention is also important. In Andy's case, he was taught that by walking up to his mother and putting his hand on her back and shoulder, instead of screaming, she would stop working for a few minutes and sit with him. Another critical feature of a functional analysis is the ability of a good clinician to offer parents or teachers a variety of options to help diminish the problem behavior.

BEHAVIORAL BASICS AND TERMINOLOGY

Although some families choose to follow a "strict" Lovaas approach, including the almost exclusive use of the therapy room with a table and chair, this traditional, intensive behavioral program also has been modified by various researchers and clinicians (Partington & Sundberg, 1998). Despite these modifications, which will be discussed later, some essential features of these behavioral programs remain constant. A brief primer of some behavioral concepts and terms, including some specific terminology often used within the context of ABA programs (e.g., mands, tacts) will be presented here. It is important to note that space constraints limit coverage to only the most basic tenets of ABA. A thorough review of ABA-type interventions is beyond the scope of this book and supports the need for well-trained behavioral consultants and psychotherapists who are open to researching and learning about new approaches to treatment.

A basic credo of ABA is focusing, almost exclusively, upon a child's behavior. Understanding a child's underlying motivation or organic problems becomes irrelevant, particularly in the early stages of treatment planning. Another basic tenet is the focus upon observable, measurable behaviors. Documentation is critical for many reasons. One is that it allows clinicians and paraprofessionals (as well as parents) to spend their time following a treatment plan rather than trying to "figure out," each session, what to do next. Another rationale is that it is easier for parents, paraprofessionals, teachers, and others (including health plan administrators) to more objectively evaluate a child's progress.

Maintaining an extensive log (e.g., a formal journal or diary) of a child's progress can also serve as a powerful motivator for highly stressed or depressed parents. Baseline data should always be taken, and videotapes of the child's behavior can be invaluable for later comparisons and observations. If personnel changes occur, a clear record and well-documented treatment plan allows for as little transitional stress as possible. Documentation also assists treatment team members and parents in supervision and troubleshooting. In cases where paraprofessionals may have limited motivation, either due to low pay rates or intrinsic factors, keeping a detailed record of work performed, and expectations of future performance, in each session also helps families and clinicians keep their program and their child progressing. In essence, documentation provides everyone involved with an additional sense of accountability.

Some common terms used in ABA (e.g., VB), which are not necessarily familiar to generalist practitioners, are "mands," "tacts," "receptives," and "intraverbals." Mands represent verbal utterances or nonverbal signals, including sign language, that indicate a child's requests or needs. One can also think of mand as shorthand for "demand." For example, a child might say "cracker" when she wants a cracker, or "I want my Mommy" when she wants her mother. She might also point at a cracker or sign "cracker" when she sees one or is hungry. Mands are considered one of the most basic and critical skills for children in ABA because they represent a first clear attempt to communicate. They also help parents and professionals identify things that can serve as positive reinforcers. Because the child identifies her own wants and desires, which have the most intrinsic value as reinforcers for positive behavior, most programs use mands as their foundation.

Another important term is "tact." A tact is something used to label or describe an object or make an observation. For example, a child may state "ball," "You have juice," or "This cookie is big." Tacts can serve as the basis for reciprocal communication as well. Receptives are often used to assess whether or not the child understands an instruction. A paraprofessional or parent may say "Look!" or "Go get your shoes." If the child is able to look where instructed, or he complies and gets his shoes, he has demonstrated receptive skills. Receptives are critical for both safety issues and in any learning environment. It is also important to note that to accomplish a receptive, children do not necessarily need to speak, as long as they follow through with the appropriate behavioral response.

Intraverbals represent a child's response (verbal or nonverbal) to a question or questions of another person. A paraprofessional may ask a child, "Tell me what you are eating?," and the child hopefully will respond, "cracker." Many programs involve children learning to answer a variety of intraverbals, including "WH" questions such as who, what, where, when and why. Answering "when" and "why" are typically more difficult because they involve some degree of abstraction and an understanding of cause-and-effect relationships. A variety of programs are available via VB to help children learn these skills.

Reinforcers vary widely among children, and they may vary widely with the same child depending upon her symptom severity and time in treatment. The best guide to the most effective reinforcer is to follow the child's lead, especially if she is able to use mands. Some children with severe autism may begin treatment with food items (primary reinforcers) as reinforcers, moving eventually to nonedible, tangible reinforcers, such as hugs, kisses, or permission to play with a special toy. The goal is for reinforcement to become more abstract and secondary, including verbal praise, smiles, or even stickers to count toward some larger reward.

SPECIALIZED TRAINING IS REQUIRED

Although many generalist practitioners may be interested in helping parents develop and implement an ABA-based program, specialized training is required. Psychologists and social workers simply cannot call themselves experts and engage in this kind of intensive behavioral therapy for both ethical and professional reasons. Also because ABA represents in-vivo therapy, many psychologists and doctoral-level therapists with primarily office-based practices may not be able to readily engage in such intensive treatment with children. Instead, generalists may find themselves helping parents gather the appropriate behavioral specialists and therapeutic support staff, and helping to oversee a program that includes realistic goals and data collection. (The *Journal of Applied Behavior Analysis* is a fine resource.)

Some universities now offer specialized graduate or certificate programs in the development, implementation, and supervision of ABA-based programs. Graduates who pass a formal examination are often referred to as Board Certified Behavior Analysts (BCBA) and less formally, or for those without specialized certification, as Behavioral Specialists, Behavior Analysts (BA), Behavioral Consultants, or Behavioral Specialist Consultant (BSC). The term BSC is commonly used. Most programs that allow graduates to sit for the BCBA examination require that participants already have a bachelor's degree. Most colleges that offer this certificate program require three to four courses, which can sometimes be completed on-line or through some combination of in-residence and web-based supervision.

There are a number of attributes to look for when selecting a BSC. The best BSC is one who has 80 or more hours of internship training. Experience provides significant benefits in excess of knowledge in this area. Family members should feel comfortable talking to their BSC and know that they can call on her for behavioral emergencies. Perhaps most significantly, families should understand why something is being done, not just how. Coming up with more than one possible intervention or approach to a specific behavioral problem (i.e., bedwetting, tantrumming) is an essential skill for a BSC.

Individuals who engage in the actual one-on-one training with a child may or may not have a specialized degree, or even a college or high school degree. Especially if money or trained personnel are unavailable, family members, including grandparents, can play a critical role. With the general exception of family members, these individuals are often referred to as paraprofessionals, therapists, or sometimes as Therapeutic Staff Support (TSS) workers. The designation TSS is more common in certain states, including Pennsylvania, but this term does not indicate any more or less training or preparation. The term "paraprofessional" is used most commonly. Ideally, such paraprofessionals are trained via formal coursework and supervised, in-vivo sessions with a child and his BSC, but many paraprofessionals are given on-the-job training by concerned and involved parents who cannot find or afford to hire a BSC.

COMMON FEATURES OF MODIFIED ABA

A key feature of any effective ABA program is the skill level and creativity of its BSC. For example, one BSC was asked to work with a four-year-old girl with severe autism. She was so averse to the presence of anyone except her mother that she would tantrum and scream, and run and hide behind furniture, when anyone came to her home. This girl, Sara, was also completely nonverbal and had no play skills. She spent most of her time in self-stimulatory behaviors like jumping and flapping. Before beginning any kind of formal discrete trial training, which represented part of their modified ABA program, the BSC actually had to use raisins, Sara's preferred food, to "lure" her into tolerating the BSC sitting closer and closer to her. It took four different sessions, one hour each, until the BSC was able to sit next to Sara. Each paraprofessional needed to follow a similar procedure. After modifying the protocol to include hugs from her mother as reinforcers, Sara eventually learned to tolerate and even appear to enjoy meeting new people at home and in restaurants and stores. The point of this anecdote with Sara, however, is to acknowledge that her BSC did not come across any kind of formal protocol for this approach in a text or journal article. This kind of work calls for quick thinking, creativity, and flexibility, often faced with a screaming, tantrumming child and often equally distressed parents or teachers.

Another critical point of this clinical anecdote with Sara is to illustrate the benefits of Natural Environment Training (NET), in which behavioral principles are applied with many people in many different settings (not just at a table and chairs) in order to promote generalized skills and learning. Many BSCs promote community-based learning as well. When a parent has a child who darts away from them across a busy parking lot or into a crowded elevator without waiting (i.e., presents danger to self; elopement risk), the entire family will clearly benefit from such training. Helping a child engage in appropriate behavior in school or day care settings is also essential. Modified ABA-style programs can use NET to great advantage. The ultimate goal is that a child not be dependent upon prompts, whether they originate from a specific paraprofessional or parent or even physical location such as a specialized table and chair. Cognitive flexibility and generalizability are essential by-products of well-conducted NET.

COMMUNICATION SKILLS AND LANGUAGE

One critical deviation from the traditional Lovaas approach is that of verbal training, sometimes referred to as ABV, promoted by Sundberg and Partington (1998). In this case, language is taught to nonverbal children with an emphasis on function of language (and making language use "fun") as opposed to the mechanics of language. Although some parents find their child's echolalia frustrating or anxiety producing (e.g., "All Tyrone does is run around and say lines from *Sesame Street*."), ABV allows such echoic behavior to be used as a stepping stone to appropriate, spontaneous speech. For a child who is completely nonverbal, parents may be instructed to talk to each other or to characters on the child's favorite video.

For the start of such a program in one family, the husband and wife joked with each other about talking to Big Bird and Cookie Monster more than talking to each other. Whenever Cookie Monster came on screen, one parent would comment, "Hey, Cookie Monster! What's Up? I want a cookie, too!" After three weeks (three long weeks, according to the parents, who received much support from their BSC), their child suddenly blurted out during the video, "Cookie Monstey!" Both parents cried with relief and praised their son profusely. According to the father, "I think we gave that kid five bowls of M&Ms because we were so excited to hear him speak!" Within a few more weeks, their child began to echo more and more language. Soon, the program progressed to mands and tacts, while the reinforcers were changed from food to secondary reinforcers and eventually removed altogether.

For children who do not respond to such a program, and fail to make any meaningful speech sounds, despite intensive intervention over many months with the help of many professionals, a picture system or sign language may be considered. Although this approach is somewhat controversial, it has helped many children and their families. Some parents and clinicians fear that if a child learns picture schedules or sign language, he will have little or no incentive to move to spoken language. However, there is limited empirical evidence to suggest that the use of visual supports inhibits a child's acquisition of language (Bondy, 2001) if significant effort is made to transition to verbal communication. The most common visual language system employed with children with autism is the Picture Exchange Communication System (PECS, Bondy & Frost, 1998).

EXTINGUISHING PROBLEM BEHAVIOR

Helping parents find a good BSC, and helping them communicate openly with the BSC, is critical (Hillman, 2006). The best BSC excels at problem solving, particularly via functional analysis (e.g., O'Neill, Horner, Albin, Sprague, Storey, & Newton, 1997) and engaging parents and paraprofessionals in appropriate behavior modification techniques. Perhaps most importantly, generalist practitioners can help parents better understand the concept of behavioral extinction, specifically in relation to their own child's problem behaviors. Although many BSCs can perform this task, some have difficulty explaining these concepts in ways that parents might readily understand. Or, a BSC may be so pressed for time that most of it is spent developing programs rather than making lengthy explanations to parents. In essence, when anyone tries to extinguish a behavior, whether this is the behavior of a person or even an animal or insect (the use of this term is not to compare a child with autism to an animal but to assure parents that this phenomenon occurs universally among all living things that engage in self-initiated behavior), the behavior will always increase before it begins to decrease. In essence, the troubling behavior targeted for extinction, such as tantrumming, will *always* get worse before it gets better.

A good BSC is also critical because many parents, including those who are well-educated or even professionals in the fields of education or psychology, often need someone else to help analyze their own and their child's behavior. Sometimes it is difficult for parents to accept, but one cannot necessarily be objective when it comes to evaluating one's own and one's child's behavior, particularly in the midst of a tantrum or other trying situation. For example, one father noted,

> You know, I'm a special education teacher myself, and it was still hard for me to do it [use ABA to extinguish a tantrum]. Sue, a behavioral specialist, had to stand there and coach me to gently put Stan on the floor when he cried, and to help me realize that by even *looking at him* as soon as he started kicking, I was actually reinforcing his behavior. I really needed her to stand there and walk me through it. I mean, I felt really stupid at first, and I can remember almost crying about it, but we did it ... After three days he stopped tantrumming and just went to bed. I couldn't believe it ... I still credit her with helping to save his life. And, it all started in my living room when she *showed* me what to do. I never could have learned that in a book.

As noted in the previous example, it becomes critical to identify and stop "hidden" reinforcers and contingencies when working to change a child's behavior. This father did not realize that by simply turning his head and looking at his son he was reinforcing the tantrum. Sue, his BSC, helped him recognize this problem by using the somewhat simple explanation that "any attention counts, even 'bad' or what we might consider 'boring' attention." Having a competent BSC help parents enact appropriate behavior is also important. The father noted previously admitted to crying after early sessions, "I remember thinking that it was just so sad, that I didn't know what I was doing, and that my son was so upset because I wouldn't hold him when he was crying ... Just to have someone there to nod at me, to let me know that I was doing this 'right,' made all the difference. I realized that even though I was a 'professional' it was OK to get help from someone else."

Another common problem encountered is when the child's own name becomes aversive. This often occurs innocently. When a child engages in an inappropriate behavior, the parent typically yells out his name, followed by a specific command or consequence, often in a loud tone of voice. Over time, if a child associates having his name called with being yelled at or having a privilege removed, the child will naturally try to avoid the parent when his name is called. If this occurs often enough, the child may even try to physically remove himself when his name is called. This situation is particularly problematic because many children, as a core symptom of autism, do not naturally respond to their own names. Often, they must be taught to self-identify and to attend. It can help when generalist practitioners reinforce the advice of a BSC who cautions that one should try to use the child's name, when yelling, only in situations involving physical danger or, conversely, when giving good feedback or hugs and kisses. Thus, the child will begin to associate his name with positive things and will actually want to pay attention to what follows, rather than to retreat or ignore the information.

THE ROLE OF GENERALIST PRACTITIONERS

The vast majority of reports of ABA programs in the literature, as well as in popular books and television shows, are quite positive. Little information is provided about difficulties that parents may experience (cf., Johnson & Hastings, 2002). There is also limited information in the literature about how traditional psychotherapists or generalist practitioners can interface with families who are engaged in formal, or informal, ABA programs to help parents thwart common barriers to treatment. Although most generalists do not or could not supervise an intensive behavioral program themselves, they can play a critical role in helping parents implement and sustain a program by helping families avoid common barriers to treatment (Hillman, 2006).

One primary barrier to treatment is the high cost of ABA (Johnson & Hastings, 2002). Although this treatment is considered the standard of care by the US Attorney General, few states in the US provide subsidies for home-based ABA programs, and it is quite difficult to find appropriately trained consultants and paraprofessionals (Johnson & Hastings, 2002). Especially in certain parts of the country, and in most of the UK, the demand for qualified consultants significantly exceeds the supply. Because paraprofessionals do not require any kind of specialized degree, and because they can be trained on the job in certain cases, some parents have been resourceful and found college students to perform those duties as part of a required internship course for their undergraduate degrees. College students in the fields of Psychology in general, Special Education, and Social Work may also serve as possibilities for recruitment. Referrals from local support groups may be helpful.

Many independent BSCs charge between $80 and $250 per hour, and paraprofessional fees often range from $7 to $20 per hour. Because many programs require 20–40 hours per week of one-on-one intervention, not including weekly parent meetings, formal documentation and charting, and supervision for paraprofessionals, costs can be very high and are typically not covered by insurance. Parents must often make difficult decisions about hiring a less-qualified consultant for more time and less money than a well-known, certified consultant (BSC) for fewer sessions per week at a significantly higher cost. Having to shunt so much of the family's income toward treatment (or taking out a second mortgage on one's home) can lead to intense anger and grief. Still other families cannot acquire enough money to fund a program and choose to run it themselves. A generalist practitioner can best help parents make difficult decisions for themselves about how to spend their money and how to manage and interpret their emotional response.

Generalists can also help parents who may experience challenging interactions with other parents of children on the spectrum. In some situations, especially within the context of rare, state-supported programs, one parent may hear, correctly or incorrectly, that one family's child was "approved" for 35 hours per week of paraprofessional services, though their own child was "approved" to receive only 20 hours per week. Although sharing information among parents is critical for both emotional support and information gathering, sometimes such news can be devastating. Some parents respond with anger and passive aggressive behaviors toward those families who receive more services. One mother of a three-year-old with autism stated, "I mean, I had to fight tooth and nail to get Marc his hours. So now Caroline [another child's mother] won't sit next to me anymore when I go to my support group meeting. Why the hell should I be made to feel guilty or like an outcast because someone else didn't get as many hours as Marc." Yet another mother, of a four-year-old with autism, noted, "I couldn't believe that Jack didn't get as many hours as James. I mean, Jack can't even talk or go to the potty, and I know that James can. I can't make sense of this. I don't know what to do." Generalist practitioners can help parents to manage such difficult interpersonal relationships.

A common problem experienced by families with ABA programs are the boundary disturbances often encountered between patient (or client), paraprofessional, and family member. Most certified consultants or BSCs are familiar with ethical issues in relation to providing such in intense, in-vivo treatment in the home. As well as parents feeling encroached upon, many paraprofessionals feel overwhelmed when a patient's parent tells her about family secrets, episodes of their own depression, or if they witness fighting between parents or parents and their children. In some cases, paraprofessionals and BSCs can make tactful suggestions that distraught parents seek counseling from a generalist practitioner. In other cases, paraprofessionals and a BSC can help parents teach their child to behave more appropriately via ABA principles (i.e., by reinforcing positive behavior).

Some parents try to acquire, inappropriately, information about other children through paraprofessionals or the BSC. Although it may seem harmless to a parent who is not schooled in professional ethics, this type of boundary disturbance may be experienced as an affront. Those seeking information may interpret professional ethics as simply a lack of trust. But a generalist can help parents cope with such privacy issues as well by explaining these ethics. In most cases, parents are so anxious about their child's progress that they want as much information as possible, from as many sources as possible. An awareness of issues that arise from one parent feeling "jealous" of another parent or child, or acting out other interpersonal dynamics, remains key.

CURRENT CONTROVERSY AND LIMITATIONS

Like virtually all treatment approaches to autism, some controversy exists regarding Lovaas-style ABA and other modified ABA approaches. There certainly are pros and cons to such intensive behavioral treatment. One concern is the high time commitment and cost. Another complaint of some parents and clinicians is that what Lovaas defined as "recovery" in his early studies (1987) may not represent what most parents or teachers would define as true recovery. Classic Lovaas programs did not necessarily target social or play skills, such as enabling children to engage in extended conversations with other people.

Another complaint is that classic Lovaas emphasizes speech articulation over speech function. In essence, some clinicians claim that children who complete Lovaas programs have robot-like speech and limited interest in social interaction and play. One BSC noted, "It's like these kids [that completed the early programs] only wanted to talk and play when they were at their little table or in their therapy room." Skill generalization did not always appear to take place. As intoned by many experts (Edelson & Rimland, 2003; McCandless, 2003), parents must also be cautioned that ABA itself is not a panacea for autism, and that it is not the only effective treatment for their child. An integrated approach, tailored to each child, serves best.

Chapter 5

Sensory integration, systematic desensitization, and exercise: promoting interdisciplinary intervention in the mind– body relationship

> John wouldn't even let me touch him. He never wanted to be held or cuddled, even if he got hurt. For two years, the only way I could touch him was when he was sleeping. I used to sneak into his room and lay down on the pillow next to him and touch his hair and his cheek. If only I knew then about his tactile sensitivity, we could have addressed it so much sooner.
>
> – Mother of five-year-old John, diagnosed with high-functioning autism

Although stereotypical and repetitive movements (e.g., hand or finger flapping) are included in the DSM-IV-TR diagnostic criteria for autism, a significant proportion of children also suffer from a variety of sensori-motor and neurological symptoms (Rapin, 1997), which unfortunately are not included in formal diagnostic criteria. It is critical that practitioners are attuned to the presence of such sensory problems because they are often misinterpreted to the detriment of affected children. They also can represent a significant source of distress to children, as suggested by reports of adults suffering from autism (Prince-Hughes, 2002), and manifest themselves as tantrums. Clinicians must take an integrative approach to both the assessment and treatment of sensorily based symptoms, and assume an active role in educating parents and teachers.

A core diagnostic feature for children with autism is their apparent inability to play. When observed at a typical neighborhood playground, many children with autism will run or walk repetitively in circles and completely ignore the slides and swings that enthrall and entertain other children. However, recent evidence suggests that this observed inability to play is not linked with mental retardation or other cognitive deficits, or even a lack of interest in functional play, but with clear physical or neurological inabilities. There is often a lack of awareness of one's body in space or enough muscle strength to play. An inability to organize sensory input, also called problems with sensory integration (SI; Ayers, 1995), coupled with hypotonia (i.e., low muscle tone), or ataxia (i.e., problems with motor coordination), are typically associated with an autistic child's inability to clasp his fingers tightly enough to hold a crayon, throw a ball, use a computer's mouse, or to even support enough weight on one leg to lift the other to climb a playground slide.

Obtaining an appropriate diagnosis and treatment from occupational and physical therapists will significantly improve the likelihood that these children will benefit from psychologically based approaches to treatment. For example, once a patient is able to gain enough muscle strength and coordination to ride a bike or throw a ball, it becomes easier to incorporate that activity into a therapeutic play date or to use it as a reinforcer in ABA. Many parents and teachers are unfamiliar with sensory integration or neurological problems, and their lack of knowledge can even exacerbate a child's symptoms. Many treatment options for such SI problems also include systematic desensitization, which clearly falls under the purview of mental health. Thus, clinicians must take an interdisciplinary approach and help guide other parents and professionals, especially in initial assessment and treatment.

Some general clues that a child may have SI or neurological problems include constant falls, walking against walls, excessive clumsiness, staring at lines and corners, toe walking, an inability to achieve general developmental milestones related to throwing or kicking a ball, as well as buttoning shirts, zipping zippers, and coloring with crayons. Other related problems and symptoms can present themselves, including a tendency to pull or rip at one's clothing, an aversion to many foods, a very limited diet, constant drooling, an apparent unwillingness or disinterest in climbing toys or playground slides, frequent fidgeting, slumped body posture, picking fights with other children, not wanting to be held, hugged, or touched, looking at things out of the corner of one's eyes, V-sitting (i.e., sitting on the floor with one's knees forward and one's lower legs splayed out with ankles by the buttocks), avoiding a variety of sounds, covering one's ears at certain sounds, constant wakening at night, not responding to stimuli or injuries typically associated with pain, and not wanting to play in sand at the beach or walk barefoot on the grass, among others.

VISUAL DISTORTIONS AND SENSITIVITIES

Although some children with autism are described as having significantly better visual than auditory perception (Rapin, 1997), many children on the spectrum do experience a variety of visual distortions and sensitivities. Consider one woman on the spectrum who reports persistent synesthesia. This thirty-year-old woman describes that all letters and numbers she encounters are experienced in various hues and colors. Some are disturbing to her, "I very much dislike the purple 'v,' the black 'j,' … and the strange polka-dotted 'x' (Anonymous, 2002, p. 94). Her description of the number five as "aquamarine blue" provided the title for Dawn Prince-Hughes' volume regarding adults' experiences with autism.

For many children who are nonverbal, it remains unclear what their exact visual experiences are, and one can only wonder how challenging it is for such children to ascertain exactly what they are looking at and to apply even basic labels in the form of language to these objects or experiences. It remains unclear how weird or distressing such synesthesia can be, especially when one does not have a consistent frame of reference or an ability to discuss one's experience with others. It also is unclear how many children with autism experience such sensory "overlapping."

Still other children with autism appear to look at certain things intently, like lines or corners, or even lights and their shadows. Yet others look at objects almost exclusively out of the corner of their eyes, with peripheral vision. One practitioner lamented, "Oh, my goodness. This one little boy I was working with did a lot of stimming with lines and corners. And, wouldn't you know it that my new office was lined with paneling!" One theory about this proclivity for lines and corners is that the child's visual perception is so poor that simple geometric figures, the most simple being a straight line, are the easiest to process. Testimony from adults on the spectrum further suggests that such visual stimming may be a result of poor visual processing.

It is also important to note that most of these children and adults, when tested, have "normal" vision. It is as though their retinas and optic nerves are working properly, but the visual processing portion of the brain itself is not functioning properly. Hyperarousal may also account for some peripheral vision preferences; when under stress, many animals look at objects out of the corner of their eyes (Hillman, 2002; Tronick, Als, Adamsen, Wise, & Brazelton, 1978). Other adults with autism describe experiencing tunnel vision when under stress (e.g., Prince-Hughes, 2002). Limiting stress, wearing tinted lenses, providing distractions, or increasing coping skills may help with this problem.

Yet other adults with autism describe facial prosopagnosia, a sensory disturbance in which faces are unrecognizable or indistinguishable from one another. Clearly, this is a neuropsychological problem that can only impair one's social life. One woman stated plaintively, "It would take me the entire year to get to know the people I was in the same class with. When I finally ... was able to recognize them, not only when they were in their seats, but also in the [hallway], the year would be over" (Anonymous, 2002, p. 21). Donna Williams described faces being so difficult to recognize because "they never remained constant" and that even recognition of everyday objects "depended on which angle you came at them. They seemed ever changing" (2003, p. 63). Another man noted, "A street entered from the south is a different (and to me unfamiliar) street than the same street entered from the north" and that the same person wearing different clothing would not be readily recognizable (Anonymous, 2002, p. 24). Thus, objects and people had to be recognized by other means, such as texture and sounds. Many adults describe identifying people by the sound of their voices or posture.

Donna Williams also expressed regret that her slower visual processing was typically interpreted by other people as a sign of intentional rudeness or anger, rather than a function of unintentionally slow processing and distorted perceptions (Williams, 2003). Such reports of distorted or slower visual processing, particularly of faces, are consistent with recent neuropsychological findings in which the amygdala and other portions of the brain responsible for facial recognition are underdeveloped or function differently among individuals suffering from autism. When asked to view a scene from a movie that featured a kissing couple, children suffering from autism were more likely to look at light switches on the wall and what the man and woman were wearing than typical children, who tended to look at the couple's faces and mouths (Klin, Jones, Schultz, Volkmar, & Cohen, 2002).

These anecdotal reports may also help explain why the vast majority of children with autism express great affinity and often obsession with the character Thomas the Tank Engine. In this animated series, the train engines are always shown with their faces "head on," and their facial expressions appear frozen for a few seconds at a time. One theory is that children with such slow processing speed or facial prosopagnosia can better recognize and begin to interpret the character's expressions. Unfortunately, there is limited research to suggest how this type of delayed or distorted processing can be changed, though occupational therapy can be helpful in fostering better visual scanning.

Clinicians can educate parents and teachers about their child's apparent disinterest in people and help dismiss traditional views that many of these children have no empathy or simply don't care about others, and occupational therapists are often a critical component of an effective treatment team. These distortions in visual processing can also help explain why many children on the spectrum are so wedded to tradition and want people and things to remain constant for as much of the time as possible. Of course, this does not mean one should cede to the wishes of a child who demands sameness, but it does suggest that understanding the basis of their needs can help shape more effective interventions and help parents tolerate their child's resistance to change.

Children who wake frequently at night may experience extreme visual sensitivity. Any amount of light at night, including a night light or a street light through a translucent blind, can cause them difficulty with transitioning to sleep. In this case, using a night mask or room darkening shades can prove vital to both parents and caregivers. Still other children may find that wearing sunglasses when outside can help them avoid sensory overload and discomfort and allow them to begin focusing on objects and people in their environment rather than ambient light in general.

It is important to note that differences in visual processing are to be expected among children with autism. Temple Grandin described "seeing in pictures," as though all of her memories were stored on videotape and could be played back in her mind at any time (1995). Some individuals who can draw the most detailed pictures may have this type of extensive visual memory, with recall at will. For those who do, this could be harnessed as a strength or coping mechanism. In contrast, Donna Williams reports having no visual memory and that it was even difficult for her to process line drawings until she was nine years old (Williams, 2003). Again, it is strongly recommended that practitioners help parents and teachers avoid stereotypical notions that all individuals with autism possess extensive visual memory, and it remains essential that therapists conduct an accurate assessment before making assumptions about a child's behavior.

AUDITORY PROCESSING AND SENSITIVITY

For many children with autism, certain sounds evoke strong and sometimes violent reactions. One five-year-old boy was so unnerved by the sound of pressure-assisted flush toilets (like the kind often found in restaurants and newer institutional buildings) that he would cover his ears, scream, and even run into a closed metal stall door at full speed in an attempt to escape the noise. Still other children with autism respond to mechanical noises such as hair dryers, hand dryers (again, often found in restaurants and institutional settings), and even fog horns with frantic attempts to avoid the sound. Some families report having difficulty going places because it is so challenging to deal with the child's anticipatory anxiety, if they know they may encounter the sound, or the child's avoidance response or related tantrum.

Such extreme sensitivity to sound often extends well beyond mechanical noises or those which may appear reasonably unpleasant to a typical child or adult. Many individuals with autism seem to possess both an uncanny sensitivity to sounds and an inability to discriminate between background noise and one "target" or primary sound or voice, despite scoring in the normal range on basic hearing tests. This kind of problem is also referred to as difficulty in discerning auditory figure-ground. Making this type of assessment is critical and can help better inform parents and teachers. For example, one adult suffering from autism describes hearing things that other people don't, including distant telephones ringing and the hum of electrical apparatus, which makes it difficult to concentrate (Anonymous, 2002).

Still other individuals on the spectrum experience the quiet buzz of most fluorescent lights (due to improperly balanced ballast tubes) as loud and annoying, to the point of being distracted and overwhelmed. It certainly doesn't help that most public schools are lit by this form of cost-efficient lighting. If a child with autism is doing poorly in such a setting, clinicians should rule out the presence of such extreme sound sensitivities. Hyperarousal may account for some of this sensitivity, and it is interesting to consider that for many psychiatric hospital patients with hyperarousal or a heightened potential for violence, it is common unit practice to turn down or turn off the lights, particularly if they are fluorescent (Hillman, 2002). It is unfortunate that many children with autism do not have this option. However, systematic desensitization, either in the context of ABA, occupational therapy, or speech therapy, can be helpful. Adults with autism describe strategies like using earplugs or a Walkman™ to help drown out extraneous noise (Prince-Hughes, 2002). However, it is important not to let these sound blockers become an additional barrier to social interaction.

A more serious problem experienced by many children and adults with autism is that of significantly delayed auditory processing, or limited auditory memory. Donna Williams described the difficulty she experienced when trying to understand what people were saying to her.

She noted that it was difficult to understand more than three sentences at a time before literally forgetting what was said before (Williams, 2003). Social interaction and learning suffer when one cannot hold more than small segments of speech in short-term memory, and also when one cannot keep up with a normal flow of conversation.

It becomes essential to evaluate children for these auditory processing delays, and to follow up with extensive speech therapy. Helping children practice verbal digit spans (i.e., repeating a series of digits from memory) can assist in building auditory memory. Although sometimes maddening to many parents and teachers, allowing a child to repeat what is said can also aid in processing information presented verbally. It is also important to note that many children with autism can read at or above their age level and still have severe auditory processing deficits. Recognizing such scatter among different skills, and sharing this information with parents and teachers, is fundamental.

The most severe form of auditory sensory problems is verbal auditory agnosia or word deafness (Rapin, 1997). In this instance, a child may not perceive speech sounds as words, but merely as any other sound, with no specific meaning or symbolic representation. An adult suffering from autism describes the experience this way, "It is kind of like what you see on those Charlie Brown specials when the teachers talk, and you hear that 'wha, wha, wha.' I mean, it just sounds like changes in volume and random noise. It took a few years for it to sink in that those noises people were making really meant anything." Unfortunately, many children with auditory agnosia remain nonverbal without extensive intervention.

TACTILE DISTURBANCES

One three-year-old boy with autism was known for kicking and biting his peers while in line at preschool. Upon closer examination of the problem, it became apparent that Jack acted out violently after his peers inadvertently jostled him while they stood in line to go to the lunchroom or to go outside to recess. Because Jack was overly sensitive to tactile stimulation, he experienced their innocent nudging and bumping as physically painful. A psychologist worked in tandem with Jack's parents and an occupational therapist to begin to desensitize him to casual touching on his arms and legs. After a few weeks of practice and reward for being touched or bumped on the arm and remaining calm, Jack was able to stand in line without causing an incident. This change in his behavior had a significant, synergistic effect. His teachers' attitude toward him improved, and peers began to encourage him to run with them at recess. Parents who were initially hesitant to let their children play with Jack outside of school soon changed their views, and Jack participated in a series of effective, therapeutic play dates.

Systematic desensitization can be invaluable when working with children who are terrified of gritty or scratchy textures. As noted previously, many individuals with autism will avoid various sensory experiences at almost any cost, such as the feel of sand or damp grass on one's bare feet. And, children who cannot articulate their experience typically tantrum. Many parents express sadness that their young child will not go on the beach during vacation (which can make for a very long vacation if no one was previously aware of this aversion), play in a sandbox, or run or even go outside in the yard. Still others refuse to finger paint, play with Lego®, or get their faces painted at birthday parties or amusement parks. Another mother lamented, "We used to call sunscreen sun-scream. It was virtually impossible to put it on him, and to go out anywhere in the summer." Sometimes parents and teachers misinterpret these sensory disturbances as disrespect for their willingness to provide a "fun" vacation or family activity, or a general disinterest in play, when this is not always the case. Once such tactile sensitivities are addressed via systematic desensitization, children can begin to learn to play, and families can begin to engage in more activities with less stress, confusion, and frustration.

Another problem related to tactile defensiveness is wearing clothing. Many adults with autism describe feeling tortured by tight or binding clothing as children and spending more time trying to avoid clothes or focusing on their discomfort than concentrating on what was going on around them or interacting with others. One way to help parents understand this sensitivity is to ask them to think of how it feels the first time they put on a turtleneck for the season, or when they break in a pair of tight-fitting shoes, and suggest they imagine feeling that way every time they get dressed. Sometimes simple but effective solutions for children include wearing loose-fitting clothing and cutting out the tags in the backs of shirts and pants.

An unfortunate but somewhat common complaint among family members of children with autism is that these children do not want to be touched, and they will fight to avoid being held, cuddled, hugged, or stroked. Some mothers report that even during infancy, their children often arched their backs or pulled their heads away in feeble efforts to avoid contact. One can only imagine the psychological trauma this inflicts upon parents. As noted at the beginning of the chapter, one mother found that the only way she could touch her child with any degree of affection was while he lay in bed, asleep. Interestingly, this child, John, was assessed by an occupational therapist at the urging of the psychologist overseeing the case.

John presented with extreme tactile defensiveness, and a variety of systematic desensitization programs were instituted, both during formal OT sessions and while at home. It also was found that John tolerated "deep pressure" much more easily than "light pressure." (Different skin receptors are involved.) John's parents learned to squeeze his shoulder firmly in affection rather than always trying to gently hold him or stroke his cheek. Also while conducting ABA, John's parents would often sit him on their laps as tolerated. Eventually, when John was approached for hugs, he would lower his head and gently "head butt" the other person rather than flail his arms or scream and tantrum. This was as much tactile stimulation as he could manage. Over the next year, he began to hug his mother with his arms out straight at his sides. She noted in her journal, "I came home from a dentist appointment to learn that John fell down while [his dad] and [his TSS worker] were working with him in the basement. He actually cried out for 'Mommy,' and reached his arms out to me when I got home. That was so cool!" Two years later, John routinely hugs his parents and "snuggles" appropriately. His mother also remarked that her own clinical depression began to abate when John began to tolerate physical contact and she could experience the affection that parents typically enjoy with their children.

KINESTHETIC AND PROPRIOCEPTIVE PERCEPTION: THE UNKNOWN SENSES

As part of the typical kindergarten curriculum, students learn about the five senses: taste, vision, hearing, smell and touch. Unfortunately, many people never learn more about the sense of "touch." In fact, to function in everyday life, individuals must possess what most people think of as "touch," including tactile perception, as discussed previously, in which they perceive textures and "surface touch." However, nerve endings deep within the muscles, tendons, and ligaments provide additional, critical information about the position of one's body, as well as the experience of deep pressure, known as proprioception. The ability to perceive the location of one's body as it moves through space, and how rapidly it is moving through that space, is another form of body perception, related to the semicircular canals and two other fluid-filled sacks in the ear, referred to as one's kinesthetic or vestibular sense (Ayers, 1995). Psychologists are already beginning to integrate aspects of OT and neuropsychology with exploration into the rapid visual-motion integration deficit in autism (Gepner & Mestre, 2002). This theory posits that children with autism who experience difficulty in processing and performing rapid movements become significantly impaired in their ability to interpret and use social cues.

Problems with any of these types of "touch" can lead to severe symptoms that may be misinterpreted as purely psychological in nature (e.g., a child has a disinterest in play rather than an actual *inability* to physically perform actions required for play), and often remain resistant to intervention. What are some symptoms or danger signs regarding problems with a child's kinesthetic or vestibular senses? Clinicians should consider the presence of excessive motor activity, such as running, jumping, climbing, bumping, and age-inappropriate biting and head banging, as well as extremely limited motor activity.

Consider four-year-old Sal, who could never sit still at preschool. He was always tapping his feet, pounding the table, or leaning back in the chair and returning it with a loud "thump." Sal literally bounced around the room and seemed to career off the walls. When bumped by other children, he would bite them, and when frustrated, he would hit his head against the wall. He also pressed his hands very hard against his temples, sometimes until he made small marks. Rather than address any potential sensory integration problems, his parents and teachers assumed that he had an "attitude problem." Further assessment, at the urging of a clinical psychologist, brought Sal and his family to treatment with a skilled occupational therapist. Sal had little sensitivity to surface pressure and craved activation of his "deep pressure" or proprioceptive receptors. Working with weighted vests and engaging in gross motor activity (e.g., bouncing on a trampoline and running) before class helped him substantially. Like Temple Grandin, who developed her own personal "squeeze machine," based upon her study of animals as a child, Sal enjoyed being wrapped up and squeezed like a "hot dog" in a lycra blanket at home. He even began to walk over to his father with the blanket and say, "Dog, Daddy!" After a few months, Sal's inappropriate behavior in class diminished; his teachers no longer regarded him as a "troublemaker," and he was better able to interact with peers and learn from his home-based ABA program.

Also consider the little boy, John, mentioned at the beginning of the chapter, who did not play on traditional playground equipment such as monkey bars and slides, but paced obsessively around the perimeter. His parents cried when he simply had no interest in his new tricycle, when all of the children his age in their neighborhood enjoyed riding theirs. Formal assessment revealed this little boy had such poor proprioceptive and vestibular skills that he had only a limited notion of where his body was in space. For him, standing on one leg while lifting the other to climb a slide, while holding onto a ladder, was simply too much to process. Standing on one leg while throwing the other over a tricycle seat was similarly too difficult.

One way to explain such proprioceptive problems to parents is to compare their child's experience to being on Novocain (R. Jensen, personal communication, September 17, 2005). Virtually all adults can relate to the feelings of frustration, embarrassment, and annoyance after receiving Novocain or another anesthetic at the dentist and then attempting to eat or drink afterwards. One mother joked, "Oh, yeah, it's like on the movie *Airplane* where the guy has the drinking problem. I was so thirsty but it all just kept rolling down my chin." Explaining that a child may have perpetually numb or "Novocain" legs could help parents understand why it is so difficult for her to run or climb stairs. Again, one enlightened parent summed up her response by saying, "Now I get it. I kept trying to make him do something that he just couldn't. He wasn't trying to piss me off or be bad, and the poor thing wasn't trying to be lazy. I'm so glad we're getting help now."

Consistent with the rapid visual-motion integration deficit hypothesis, the child discussed earlier, John, intensely disliked movement. It was as though he would resist movement of almost any kind, and thus, resist almost all types of play. He had no alternative play skills to call upon, and his self-selected stim behaviors (in this case, staring at lines and flipping light switches) became even more entrenched. Occupational therapy helped significantly, and included activities that encouraged movement and proprioceptive (i.e., body) awareness, such as building up a tolerance for being in a swing that rocked gently, and learning to stand and move one leg purposefully at a time. His parents also learned to work along with this little boy to slowly guide him as he climbed a ladder, placing his feet securely on the rungs, and then helping him on to the slide. Over time he began to enjoy going to the playground.

It is important to inform parents and teachers that well-conducted OT sessions often look like pure play. Because treatment is often taxing or stressful, especially if one experiences sensory distortions, the best occupational therapists use distraction and humor to engage their patients. It is also important to advise others about this practice because some individuals close to the child may balk at treatment and resist it because it doesn't seem "scientific" enough, or they may report feeling that they are "paying a lot of money for [Chris] to just have fun." Although it may seem outside of the purview of a mental health practitioner, the need for interdisciplinary treatment is vital, and all applicable avenues must be considered.

Upon closer examination, additional oddities of movement are often seen among children suffering from autism. Dawn Prince-Hughes (2002), an adult diagnosed on the autistic spectrum, described how the feel of the ground itself was repellant to her, and that it played a large part in her experience of toe walking. Some children may resist becoming left-handed or right-handed or they may appear not to develop good skills with either hand. Other children are unable to engage in "midline crossing," in which one hand or arm (or leg) literally cannot reach across the other side of the body. The best way to explain this is to imagine a child sitting in front of a pile of blocks, and that the child is right-handed. On the child's left is a purple polka-dotted block. The child wants this block badly, and she wants to put it in a small bucket on her right side. However, the child reaches out slowly and awkwardly with her left hand to grab the block. Then she slowly brings her left hand to the middle of her body where she grabs the block with her right hand, and proceeds to use her right hand to drop the block into the bucket. (She is unable to reach across her body with her right hand to grab the purple block.) When one knows what to look for, seeing a child conduct such a complicated series of steps with two limbs to perform what should be one fluid action with one limb is both riveting and disturbing. Imagine how many times a day typical children and adults reach across their bodies to grab or manipulate things, without even thinking about doing it. If one is working so hard to "plan" and execute even the most simple movements, how can there be much psychic energy or concentration left over to engage in social activity or cognitive skills?

With such children, it is as though only one hemisphere of the brain is working at a time, and that one is neglectful of the other (also consider drawings of stroke patients with unilateral or visuospatial neglect; their movements are similar; Marshall, Lazar, Binder, Desmond, Drucker, & Mohr, 1994). Such an inability to grab and use everyday objects will severely limit play, and this is often overlooked by most professionals who work with children with autism. As noted, parents and teachers (and even other practitioners who may be unaware of sensory integration disorders) are likely to make inappropriate attributions for these children's behavior, and regard them as clumsy, lazy or, even worse, mentally retarded. Practitioners can provide a vital source of early screening, and get these children into appropriate, and often interdisciplinary, treatment.

HYPOTONIA AND ITS MANIFESTATIONS

Low muscle tone or hypotonia can present itself in unexpected ways. Although the cause of such low muscle tone is unclear (it has been associated with anoxia and mercury toxicity; Bernard, Enayati, Redwood, Roger, & Binstock, 2001), poor proprioceptive perception could lead to a self-perpetuating, vicious cycle. Not receiving proper input about the body's location in space is likely to lead to additional inactivity, which contributes to further low muscle tone. Some warning signs to consider for hypotonia include excessive drooling, slumping in one's chair, constantly changing positions in one's chair, an inability to blow out birthday candles, or to blow one's nose, avoiding coloring, coloring or drawing in very light strokes, a disinterest in small blocks or toys, and not dressing oneself.

Consider four-year-old Ricky, who would sit passively at preschool and avoid interacting with peers. He would sit in his seat at school without getting up or being disruptive, but by the end of the day, he seemed to become a human pretzel, leaning in his chair, slumping in his chair, and even kneeling in his chair. Although he did not actively disrupt the classroom or engage in aggressive behavior, Ricky was unable to concentrate or learn in school. He also tended to roll his pencil on his desk or twirl it, rather than attempt to write. When the teacher's aide insisted that Ricky spend extra time practicing his coloring and writing, he would often tantrum and cry. He soon began protesting about going to school. His mother was frustrated that he couldn't seem to get dressed in the morning. He always wanted someone to pull up his pants and put on his shoes. Upon hearing this, his teacher wondered if Ricky was lazy or even mentally retarded. After careful assessment, it became clear that Ricky was suffering from hypotonia. He simply did not have the muscle strength to sit for long periods of time, and his inability to get dressed did not stem from laziness, but from the lack of finger and arm strength necessary to grab and hold onto a waistband and pull hard enough to pull up a pair of pants. Holding, guiding, and pressing on a pencil was even more difficult. It is alarming how debilitating this condition can be, and how it is regularly overlooked and misdiagnosed.

It is challenging for many typical adults to understand how low muscle tone could be related to problems sitting. After all, most of these children appear physically normal. However, it can be helpful to ask parents and teachers, as well as other individuals who work with the child, to consider how they would feel if they were asked to sit at a bar stool all day to do their work. Instruct them to think about how it feels to sit high up on a perch with no back support and only a small rail to rest their feet. Would they begin to fatigue? Would they fidget? Would they just give up? Would they be able to concentrate? When put in this context, many individuals grasp the concept quickly. Lay persons and others working with children must recognize that increased muscle tone only occurs with the large "trunk" muscles first (e.g., abdominal, back, thighs, and shoulder muscles), and that strength and skill with smaller muscles and fine motor skills come only after the "core" of the body is stabilized. In essence, until a child has enough trunk stability to sit for long periods of time, he cannot hope to begin to learn to color or cut with scissors. Too much energy and concentration is being used for sitting.

It also is helpful for parents, teachers, and therapists to assure that when children are engaged in other therapies, they have suitable tables and chairs for their size. For example, one child who was losing weight due to an apparent disinterest in eating was actually diagnosed with hypotonia. Sitting in a high kitchen chair, his feet couldn't touch the floor. This little boy became so fatigued from balancing himself on his chair that he didn't have enough energy to sit and eat with silverware. Because he had only limited verbal skills, he could not articulate this problem to his parents. When he was given a chair with a stack of books under his feet, he began eating more quickly, and he ate more food overall. Soon his weight caught up with that of his peers. His teachers at school were also instructed to make sure that he had foot support, and his participation in various table activities improved as well.

Another point for all treatment team members to consider is that if a child presents fine motor deficits (e.g., with writing or coloring), making her practice over and over is not always going to help. If the child suffers from hypotonia, as the child described earlier, such forced practice sessions are going to fatigue her to the point where she becomes resistant to the activity and does nothing to foster true fine motor skills. Trunk control and strength must be mastered first. It is like telling someone with a sprained elbow to practice coloring and press harder on the paper. Of course, this concept can be difficult for parents and teachers to understand. It can be helpful to explain to others that even Olympic swimmers have adopted this truism. Strengthening the trunk and postural muscles of affected children can be accomplished via occupational therapy and a variety of at-home activities. Crab walking and learning to play while lying on one's stomach for a few minutes at a time can be accomplished easily and integrated into a family's routine with limited disruptions and no extra costs.

To encourage the development of fine muscle control, children may be asked to find and remove coins from a mound of therapy putty or Play Dough. One mother described with some fondness, "Cory couldn't use his fingers very well. When his trunk started getting better, we would go to the mall and I would bring along a bunch of pennies. He liked throwing them in the fountain, so I would place my palm out, flat, the way the OT showed me, and he would have to use a 'pincer grasp' to grab and pick up the coin. He couldn't always throw hard enough to get them in the fountain every time, either, but we really enjoyed it. It was sad in a way, but it was much more like fun than therapy or some kind of exercise." Mental health providers conducting ABA or social groups can consult with an OT to develop appropriate, beneficial, and fun activities, like the above, in work with their own patients.

Hypotonia can also help account for some of the difficulty in verbal skills among children on the spectrum. For children who drool constantly due to low muscle tone, even moving one's mouth to speak can be taxing. Sometimes occupational therapists will have children blow bubbles or feathers or cotton balls on tabletops to help strengthen those muscles. Still others recommend having children drink out of a straw to exercise those muscles because it takes significantly more effort and muscle strength than drinking out of a cup. Increasing muscle tone around the mouth, face and neck can be an essential step in helping many children begin to speak, or to speak for longer periods of time.

It is recommended that children with autism who are generally non-verbal be tested for apraxia, a condition in which the brain does not provide muscles with the right instructions to move to make speech sounds. This is qualitatively and quantitatively different than hypotonia, in which the proper neural messages are being sent, but the muscles cannot carry them out, or can only do so for limited periods of time. Of course, apraxia and hypotonia may coexist, requiring even more intensive intervention. On a practical level, a diagnosis of apraxia can provide parents with reimbursement options from insurance companies, who often flatly refuse to pay for services related directly to autism or other developmental disabilities.

EXERCISE AND AUTISM

Emergent research from Neuropsychology also provides exciting and compelling reasons for therapists to entice children suffering from autism (and their families) to exercise. Recent findings suggest that as little as an hour of aerobic activity a week can lead to a significant decline in depression and anxiety. A groundbreaking study that specifically employed children with autism showed that one hour a week of exercise, even in the form of unstructured running and jumping, led to significant decreases in self-stimulatory behavior and aggressive acts, as well as measurable increases in academic performance (Kern, Koegel, Dyer, Blew, Fenton, 1982; Lochbaum & Crews, 1995). Sometimes as little as 15 minutes of vigorous activity per day conveyed significant benefits.

Educating parents about the value of even the most simple interventions, such as unstructured running and jumping, is essential. Many parents are overjoyed when they learn that spending time romping with their child is helpful for everyone. One father stated, "My god. Here is something he likes to do anyway, and I don't have to feel like every minute he's got to be sitting in a chair or 'learning' something or going to some special therapy. It seems like that's all we do anyway ... It takes away a little guilt about wanting some 'time off' [for playing and exercising] that is still good for him." Parents of children with sensory issues should not feel guilty, though, if their children do not automatically like to run and jump due to hypotonia or other problems; with proper OT and perseverance, that time will come. Working in an interdisciplinary treatment team that includes occupational therapists as well as mental health providers certainly can have its benefits.

Chapter 6

Addressing core social deficits

Self-reports of many individuals with autism suggest that they have a deep-seated desire for friendship, but that they somehow do not know how to forge or foster friendships. Fortunately, researchers and clinicians are beginning to develop interventions to address this crucial area of development.

It is relatively easy to articulate whether a child suffering from autism demonstrates significant progress in diminishing the frequency of stim behavior and tantrums, or increases his frequency of word usage. However, assessing and promoting positive outcomes in terms of social functioning appears more complicated. For example, one parent relates:

Ok. So Deon is five now. We've been doing ABA and OT and stuff, and we've treated a lot of his medical problems. Now he talks, he tells me he loves me, he plays with toys, he sits still most of the time at school, he doesn't really tantrum any more, and a lot of people who meet him for the first time, briefly, don't have any idea he has autism. But something is missing. It's like he still doesn't get excited about things, or about being around other kids. He'd still rather play by himself, and he doesn't really look at me when I'm talking. He gets invited to birthday parties, especially if everyone in his preschool class gets invited, but the phone doesn't ring for play dates. It's kind of sad. I mean, I'm thrilled about the progress we've made so far, but there's still a lot that's wrong, even if he's not biting or kicking anymore. It's like Deon still isn't "all there yet" and no one can tell us what to do. I mean, how can you make a kid learn to have friends?

Still other parents describe horrific and bizarre situations in which they experienced severe emotional trauma or physical injuries themselves, and their child with autism laughed or ignored them when they were in obvious distress or pain: "It was as though I wasn't there; I was just like a piece of furniture. He didn't need me for anything at that moment, so it was like my crying was just some kind of weird background noise to him. Looking back on it now, it still makes me feel nauseous, just thinking about it. I was so angry with Josh, but at the same time so scared. Who was this child? Is he somehow a monster or an alien? When he acts like that, I wonder if he will ever really be able to make it in this world." This mother's concern is consistent with recent studies that suggest strongly that social competence is a highly significant predictor of one's success in life (cf., Gutstein & Whitney, 2002).

A longitudinal study of preschoolers (without any type of specialized intervention) found that those children suffering from autism displayed marked impairments in social functioning throughout adolescence (Sigman & Ruskin, 1999). Other researchers studied the friendships of adolescents with autism and deemed them generally devoid of feelings of security and companionship (Bauminger & Kasari, 2000). Self-reports of adults with autism often describe an indifference to friendship or deep-seated, unmet needs for understanding and companionship (e.g., Prince-Hughes, 2002). Thus, one of the most important, emergent areas in the field of autism is the development of various therapeutic programs and activities designed to increase child-driven or self-initiated social interaction and communication.

THEORY OF MIND

A basic knowledge of the core social deficits in autism is critical, including the often touted "Theory of Mind" (TOM; Baron-Cohen, Ring, & Wheelwright, *et al.*, 1999), in which typical children and adults are able to imagine themselves in the mind of, or take the perspective of, another person in order to foster empathy, inform their social responses, or simply gather information about an ambiguous or novel situation. For neurotypical children, TOM skills appear to be functional by age four. Deficits in TOM have been referred to as "mind blindness" and an inability to engage in "mind reading" (e.g., Gladwell, 2005). TOM helps speakers realize when their counterpart is becoming bored over a prolonged discussion of stock picks, in the case of adults for example, or favorite dinosaurs or cars, in the case of children. TOM is also linked to spontaneous, combined attention and social referencing, in which typically developing children look at the faces of adults (and later peers) in ambiguous situations to gather critical information.

Deficits in TOM are likely to lead to an absence of pretend or symbolic play (Rutherford & Rogers, 2003) and impaired empathy (Baron-Cohen, 1988). Anecdotal evidence suggests that many children and adults on the autistic spectrum are quite gullible. Due to an inability to consider that another person may have a different point of view, it does not occur to many individuals with autism that someone else would have any reason or need to lie, cheat, or steal. Many of these same individuals also are quite inflexible, moralistic, and rule-bound (Grandin, 1995); it is difficult or impossible for them to imagine another's extenuating circumstance. Because so many children with autism can appear naïve, clinicians and parents should exercise caution that these children be well protected from the potential ill motives or schemes of others. Without intervention, it is unlikely that these children would learn from the "mistakes" committed by others. Conversely, it can represent a real milestone in treatment when a child with autism actually begins to lie. Typical children lie, in part, because they realize that they can influence others to have a more favorable, alternative viewpoint.

Various symptoms of autism may be linked to deficits in TOM. With the exception of slapstick physical comedy, humor and sarcasm are generally lost on individuals suffering from autism. At its most basic core, humor involves the interpretation of some event or statement from two perspectives, and the conclusion that they are somehow incongruous or inappropriate. Many children with autism hear a joke, and when others laugh, they might often state, "But, that's not funny!" Learning to appreciate humor or things that are "silly" can represent a real turning point in treatment.

The common experience of idiosyncratic speech may be associated with deficits in TOM. For example, one four-year-old with autism kept telling his mother, "Your mother and father are coming over to dinner." When he was told that he should say, "My grandmother and grandfather are coming over to dinner," he responded angrily, "No, they're not!" Although this boy seemed to show an initial grasp of another's perspective, that of his mother's relationship to his grandmother and grandfather, it was as though he could not maintain both viewpoints or concepts at one time.

NEUROPSYCHOLOGICAL ANALYSES OF ATTENTIONAL GAZE

With the use of computer-assisted eye-tracking methodology in various experiments, valuable insight has been gained into factors associated with deficits in TOM. In their often-cited study, Klin and colleagues (Klin, Jones, Schultz, Volkmar, & Cohen, 2002) found that among fifteen adolescent boys suffering from autism, compared to a sample of matched, typical controls, the boys with autism were significantly more likely to look at other people's mouths, rather than their eyes, when talking. This study also suggests that, for children suffering from autism, the expressions on other people's faces appear to be given the same importance and level of emotional excitement as the color of a cup or placement of a light switch in the same room. The parts of the brain typically responsible for eliciting emotional arousal when looking at faces, including the amygdala, do not function as well among children with autism when presented with social stimuli (e.g., Baron-Cohen *et al.*, 1999). The boys with autism in Klin's study were also more likely to spend time fixating on objects in the background or on parts of people's bodies than faces. In fact, the best predictor of whether or not a boy could be identified as belonging to the autistic or typical group was eye contact. A tendency to look at people's faces and mouths, rather than inanimate objects in the environment, was associated with better daily adjustment and social competence.

One explanation for why the boys with autism spent less time looking at others' eyes than their mouths is offered by the rapid visual-motion integration deficit hypothesis (Gepner & Mestre, 2002), which posits that individuals with autism have severe motion-processing delays and sensory integration disorders in which they find rapidly moving stimuli aversive. Avoidance of movement, of both self and other, becomes automatic and pervasive. Because saccadic eye movements are among the fastest movements performed by the human face, it makes sense that the autistic adolescents' gazes gravitated toward nonmoving inanimate objects and the slower movements of other people's mouths rather than their eyes. Due to such processing difficulties, significantly valuable social information can easily be missed, especially when critical visual-facial cues often manifest themselves only in milliseconds (Elkman & Friesen, 1978). With facial prosopagnosia (e.g., Barton, Cherkasov, Hefter, Cox, O'Connor, & Manoach, 2004) or "blindness," in which faces themselves do not appear as one discrete, meaningful unit, one can only imagine how difficult it is for children suffering from autism to function in any social setting.

MIRROR NEURONS AND THEIR ROLE IN IMITATION

Emergent research regarding "mirror neurons," first discovered in 1995 (Rizzolatti, Camarda, Gallese, & Fogassi), also suggests that abnormal metabolic activity in a specific region of the brain is associated with TOM deficits, like those commonly observed in autism (Williams, Whiten, Suddendorf, & Perrett, 2001). Mirror neurons, located in the prefrontal cortex, are also referred to as "monkey see, monkey do" neurons (Carey, 1996). In other words, these neurons fire when an individual engages in some motor activity. They also fire when observing another person engage in motor activity. This plays a central role in allowing others to imitate things and learn new behavior, with "practice" starting mentally rather than physically (Oberman *et al.*, 2005). In addition to facilitating physical actions, mirror neurons also appear to foster the development of shared experiences and empathy. For example, when someone watches another person hit his thumb with a hammer or suffer some type of physical injury, the typical response of the other person is to wince or draw in her breath sharply in anticipation of the other's pain. Anyone who watched Gregory Louganis hit his head during the platform dive competition of the 1988 Olympics can probably remember her own automatic, empathic response at his moment of injury.

Mirror neurons are implicated in social contagion, including the tendency of others to engage in fits of shared laughter (Hatfield, Cacioppo, & Rapson, 1994). Statements from typical adults demonstrate this phenomenon: "Oh, my god. His laughter was just contagious. He was laughing so hard and then I couldn't stop [laughing] either! I could hardly catch my breath and the tears came. It was so funny and it got to the point where we were just laughing over us laughing!" This type of automatic, shared experience leads to greater empathy, which probably serves our social functioning as a larger society. These findings also suggest that among typical children, empathy may be "hardwired" to facilitate skill acquisition and social competence (cf., Wolf, Gales, Shane, & Shane, 2001). Unfortunately, children with autism do not appear to have the same level of functioning with their mirror neurons. Very rarely do children with autism notice their peers laughing and spontaneously break into laughter or spontaneously try to infer what is bringing their peers joy. Studies show that for these children on the spectrum, motor neurons fire when they engage in their own bodily movement and actions, but not in response to the movements or affective displays of others (Wolf *et al.*, 2001). Such problems with movement itself, cognitive processing, and even brain function (e.g., Baron-Cohen *et al.*, 1999) can thus pose significant barriers to the development of TOM.

A variety of "tests" exist to assess a child's TOM, and most are geared toward children between the ages of four and six. Although there are a wide variety of these tests, the "Sally-Anne" version appears commonly in the literature. To administer this test, a child is seated and asked to listen to an examiner. The child is shown two dolls, named Sally and Anne. With the help of the examiner, "Sally" puts a marble in a small basket and then leaves the room. "Anne" then takes the marble out of the basket and places it in a small box. The child is asked, "Where would Sally look for the marble when she comes back into the room?" A correct response is scored if the child responds, "in the basket." Most children with autism incorrectly respond, "in the box," failing to acknowledge Sally's differing perspective.

In another test of TOM, called the "Smarties" false belief test (Perner, Frith, Leslie, & Leekman, 1989), a child is shown a box of candy and is asked to identify what is inside. In the study report, all children questioned responded, "candy." Afterwards, the box was opened, and the children were shown a pen hidden inside. Then the children were asked what another child, who had never seen the box before, would think is inside. A correct answer would be scored as "candy." Many children with autism and PDD-NOS fail to recognize the differing perspective of another and cite "a pen" for their answers. One benefit of the Smarties test, as well as most other tests of TOM, is that these tasks are quite simple to administer, and the results are often plain for parents, teachers, or others who may need motivation to accept that their child has some kind of diagnosis or difficulty.

Interestingly, some individuals with autism perform quite well on standard TOM tests. However, they do not appear to perform well socially in spontaneous or naturalistic settings. Possible reasons advanced for this discrepancy include the fact that most social situations do not require one specific, dichotomous answer. Typical social interactions occur on a continuum, and require constant change and adaptation, and a fluid, complex response rather than a one-word reply. Still another issue is that a child with autism may not recognize, spontaneously, the social demand in a situation unless directly asked to acknowledge and consider it (see Klin, 2000, for a review). This is consistent with recent empirical studies of empathy, in which adults with autism expressed negative emotions upon learning they had upset someone. The adults with autism had no idea what they said or did that may have upset the other person. Without making their own actions salient, these individuals were completely unaware of their social role in a given situation (Baron-Cohen & Wheelwright, 2004). Anecdotal reports from adults suffering from autism also mirror these empirical reports. One young woman reported, "I had no idea that I offended people by the things I said. I never meant to do it, it just seemed to happen. And ... then most of the time I had no idea what I did, even when they told me I did something stupid."

AUTOMATIC VERSUS CONSCIOUS PROCESSING

A brief review of typical and atypical social development also is important in terms of diagnostic issues and intervention. In the first month of life, typically developing infants show a strong preference for human faces compared to inanimate objects. By nine months, typical children look at the face of a parent or caretaker to gain important information about an ambiguous situation. At this age, typical children will also point or gesture at something of interest as an interpersonal signal to others. The child will often check the face of the caregiver to gain some information or to communicate a need or desire. Social referencing or social learning, in which a child points out something or looks to another person's face for feedback, and experience sharing, in which a child looks to another simply for the sake of shared pleasure (Gutstein & Whitney, 2002), are similar constructs. One hypothesis about these generally universal activities is that somehow the child "knows" that the other person will be able to acknowledge and take his own perspective. In essence, this represents the typical child's first acknowledgment that others exist and that they may have different perspectives and viewpoints. The typical child is purported to acknowledge, cognitively, the standpoint of the other person. In contrast, a child with autism will not point at something, but literally grab the hand of a caretaker and pull her to the desired object, using her in an impersonal manner, like a tool, rather than engaging that person in some kind of shared experience. It is as though the person does not exist in terms of the child's own perspective or emotional state; no joy is found in shared discovery or information exchange. Other people are simply a means to an end.

One aspect of controversy regarding this process of pointing and shared attention among typical children, which is described as a necessary precursor to TOM, is the supposition that this activity is largely automatic and unconscious rather than pedantic or purposeful (Williams, 2004). In fact, some researchers suggest that this process of gathering information from and about others' emotional states occurs primarily as a right hemisphere activity – without the use of language. In support of this hypothesis, the orbitofrontal and medial temporal circuit in the right hemisphere appears to play a significant role in the interpretation of others' facial expressions (Sabbagh, 2004). Gladwell (2005) posits that when neurotypical adults are overwhelmed with external and internal stimulation, often as a result of increased heart rates and heightened physiological arousal (e.g., during a high-speed police chase), they lose the ability to make rapid, unconscious, nonverbal judgments about people's behavior and motives, becoming "automatically autistic." In other words, subjects who are asked to undergo the Sally-Anne task do not necessarily think through their response in words; they simply "know it" somehow via the right hemisphere. Additional research with neurotypical adults suggests that many effective judgments about others' emotional states and our own preferences for certain foods and consumer goods can become clouded when an individual is asked to think about or labor over decision making. It is as though using the left hemisphere, including the language center of the brain, detracts from this automatic processing (Schooler, Ohlsson, & Brooks, 1993).

Because many individuals with autism appear to experience significant problems integrating their own sensory experiences, it follows that many are in a consistently high state of arousal. It then makes sense to assume that their ability to use the right hemisphere to automatically interpret others' emotional states from visual and other nonverbal cues becomes impaired. Additionally, adults with autism describe having to use significant amounts of time and energy to think through or process their own social interactions, including the expressions and statements from other people. (The left medial frontal regions of the left hemisphere of the brain appear to allow one to reason or think about others' mental states; Sabbagh, 2004.) One adult woman with autism stated plaintively, "It is just exhausting to function socially," especially when the numbers of individuals present increase (Anonymous, 2002).

Because the brain function of children with autism appears different from that of typical children, it also follows that TOM is not "automatic" for them. Instead, their entire social repertoire appears dependent upon their ability to consciously gather the correct information, compare it to previous experience (e.g., Loddo, 2003), and then interpret it. Impaired auditory and visual processing skills can also compound this problem. Children suffering from autism also tend to have difficulty initiating intentional behavior (Noens, van Berckelaer, & Ina, 2005), which would include the need to initiate and sustain a lengthy perceptual and cognitive process to decipher dynamic and complex interpersonal inter-actions; this can represent a social crisis.

Unfortunately, clinicians do not currently have a wealth of options available regarding possible social skill interventions. Most strategies for addressing specific social deficits have been in use for less than a decade. A number of researchers report that some children with autism can be taught or "trained" to succeed at various false belief tasks. How-ever, such interventions have proven problematic because they provide only limited generalizability to other, more fluid social settings (e.g., Okuda & Inoue, 2000). Available methodologies that focus on social skills for children suffering from autism include Social Stories, social groups, and Relationship Development Intervention (RDI; Gutstein, 2000). Each method will be discussed in turn, with a focus upon the em-pirically measured outcomes of these approaches. The need to develop and assess effective social skills interventions must be emphasized, particularly within the context of educational programming (Strain & Schwartz, 2001).

SOCIAL STORIES

In the mid 1990s, Carol Gray introduced Social Stories as a way of help-ing children with autism learn how to play simple games with other child-ren as an introduction to the social world (1994; 2000). Social Stories are simple, easy-to-read stories constructed specifically for one child, targeting a specific upcoming event or situation. The story is constructed in the first person and is typically ten pages or so in length. The vocabu-lary is tailored to the child in question, and line drawings or photographs often accompany the text. Social Stories are intended to provide child-ren with autism with specific information about what, where, when, how, and why things are supposed to happen, and with whom; these statements are referred to as descriptive sentences. Social Stories are also intended to include information about how other people may be thinking or feeling (known as perspective statements), and provide clear guidelines and expectations for how the child is expected to act in return (known as directive statements). These informational booklets are also meant to feature a specific ratio of one directive sentence for every two to five descriptive or perspective sentences. This ratio is limited so that the child does not become overwhelmed with too many directions.

Gray (1994; 2000) suggests that if the child can read, it is best for him to read the story to himself at least once a day until the social skill set is mastered. If a child cannot read, the social story can be read to him (e.g., Scattone, Wilczynski, Edwards, & Rabian, 2002). Sometimes it is practical for the story to be stapled or bound and laminated. Some children like the stories so much that they become like a toy. For children with sensory integration deficits or hypotonia, laminated pages may also be easier to turn. Subjects of Social Stories are vast, and may include information about reducing disruptive behaviors, such as staring inappropriately at women, shouting, or tipping one's chair in school (e.g., Scattone *et al.*, 2002); increasing the frequency of desired behavior, such as playing with other children at school (Barry & Burlew, 2004); eating lunch, and greeting peers (e.g., Rowe, 1999); and preparing for novel situations (e.g., Ivey, Heffin, & Alberto, 2004), such as trips to the dentist, going swimming, or even playing with a new toy at a therapy session or in school.

There are a number of obvious benefits to using Social Stories. They can be created by parents, teachers, therapists, physicians, or virtually anyone involved in the child's life. Their construction generally takes less than one hour, and they are cost-effective. The time it takes to administer this intervention is also minimal. Additionally, aspects of an autistic child's symptoms may actually foster their use. For example, because many children with autism are rule-bound and adhere to rituals, adoption of such social schemas may be easily accomplished and followed. The visual nature of the Social Stories may also appeal to children who are more likely to process visual information better than verbal instructions (Scattone *et al.*, 2002). A specially trained clinician is not required for administration. By ethical standards, Social Stories are inherently unobtrusive and noninvasive. Face validity is high, which may help some parents and teachers who balk at other, less "obvious" interventions (such as discrete trials) adopt Social Stories more readily into their child's treatment plan.

When Gray first presented her Social Story intervention strategies in the early 1990s (Gray & Gerand, 1993; Gray, 1994), limited empirical evidence was available to support their use. In recent years, however, a significant body of research has accumulated to suggest that Social Stories are effective in producing increases in specific, desirable behaviors, decreases in specific, nondesirable behaviors, and increases in participation in upcoming, novel events (e.g., Ivey *et al.*, 2004). Parents and therapists themselves often describe their use as pleasurable (Smith, 2001). One mother of a six-year-old with autism noted, "It's just like a bedtime story. It's fun, he will now tolerate sitting on my lap to read, and I know it's helping him."

However, there are limitations to the use of Social Stories. If a child with autism cannot read and is limited in the comprehension of speech, it is obviously unclear how effective such Social Stories may be. It is unclear how many presentations of each story are necessary to elicit behavioral change, and how effective these interventions are in the long term, and no longitudinal studies exist, to date, that address these questions. It also remains unclear what proportion of the children subject to this intervention find it pleasurable. Some studies note that, while effective in reducing problematic behavior, some children remained resistant to the intervention (Scattone *et al.*, 2002). The most serious drawback with Social Stories is that their use does not appear to allow for significant generalization across social settings or for related target behaviors. For example, although Ivey and colleagues (2004) were successful in helping children with autism become more engaged in novel activities in their speech therapy group, the children in their study did not automatically know or learn to ask others for help or directions. Unfortunately, a review of all outcome studies available regarding Social Stories also showed that none included measures of treatment generalizability (Sansosti, Powell-Smith, & Kincaid, 2004).

Ivey *et al.* (2004) assert that one Social Story may be needed for each specific social skill. This suggests that good Social Stories follow from a clear task analysis, in which all aspects of a task are identified (Englemann & Carnine, 1982) and taught, including those that may seem implicit or obvious to neurotypical peers. In other words, it may not be as simple to write good Social Stories as one may initially believe. Care must be taken not to overlook any aspect of the situation, including likely responses from others. This concern is mirrored in the self-report of one adult male with autism, Daniel, who described his own experience with a "self-written" social story. He stated, "I figured out that if I smile a little bit, but not a lot, nod my head, and say, 'Mm, hm,' that I will be OK, even if I have no idea what to say or what the other person is really talking about." Such scripts may allow an individual with autism to "pass" in the neurotypical social world, but with some inherent limitations.

It is recommended that clinicians not limit their social skills interventions to Social Stories alone (also see Sansosti *et al.*, 2004). Clinicians should prepare parents to be on guard for school programs or state-assisted agencies whose directors may focus upon Social Stories exclusively due to their limited costs. Although useful, Social Stories must be part of a series of social skills interventions in order to have any hope of fostering cognitive flexibility and generalizability across settings.

SOCIAL SKILL GROUPS

Another emergent intervention for social skills is that of social skills training or therapy groups. Most groups typically comprise five to twelve children on the spectrum and may be led by Psychologists, Behavioral Specialists, Speech Therapists, and Occupational Therapists. The basic premise of these groups is that children can be taught social skills within the context of an actual social setting, with other peers. Parents may or may not be invited to view the group through a one-way mirror or from across the room. Because of the lack of therapeutic services available in most communities, these types of groups also allow more children to receive treatment at a typically lower cost to their families.

Most social skills groups incorporate some type of structure in their programming. They may last from 30 minutes to an hour, depending upon the children's age and attention span. "Hello" songs are often used to start the group, and some type of semistructured activity usually follows that requires turn taking or conversation (e.g., playing a game; engaging in some type of gross motor activity; doing a craft), perhaps followed by some kind of psycho-educational information and practice regarding conversation or manners, and finally, some type of "good-bye" song or story to end the session. Formal curricular goals may include emotion recognition, perspective taking, problem solving (e.g., Solomon, Goodlin-Jones, & Anders, 2004), conversational skills, greetings, play skills, and fine and gross motor skills.

One theoretical basis for these groups is that of social modeling (Bandura, 1971), in which children learn skills by watching others engage in similar activities. As a caveat, care must be taken that children enrolled in these groups are able to engage in simple imitation, at least some of the time. Positive reinforcement is also critical. Children are first rewarded by their therapists, and later by their peers, for appropriate behavior. Some group leaders also employ token economies, like stickers and prizes, or later, less concrete reinforcers such as claps, hugs, and smiles. Interdisciplinary group leaders are often used because many professionals note that when children on the spectrum are asked to engage in gross or fine motor skills, as required for most types of typical play, their conversational and concentration skills become impaired due to the additional demands placed upon them by the movement. Thus, professionals can help scaffold the children's speech and social interaction during such physical activities. A small child to teacher/therapist ratio is also essential to learning. Children can receive more attention from therapists, and it is often easier for children suffering from autism to focus their attention on a few people rather than many. This is consistent with many adults with autism who describe becoming overwhelmed socially when even more than one other person is involved (Anonymous, 2002).

For greater effectiveness, social skill interventions appear to require various components. Kransny and colleagues articulate five essential aspects (Kransny, Williams, Provencal, & Ozonoff, 2003). First, the intervention must include a careful, systematic task analysis that distills complex social interactions into smaller, concrete steps that can be memorized and applied in a variety of settings. Second, it must address the child's likely deficits in language. Third, the intervention must focus upon interactions with peers. Fourth, it must include practice in naturalistic settings, and fifth, it must include parents and teachers to promote continuity. One benefit of including parents in the group, even as observers, is that it may reduce depressive symptoms, particularly among mothers (Solomon *et al.*, 2004). Parents should be advised to seek out social skills groups that incorporate as many of these aspects as possible.

Unfortunately, little outcome research exists regarding such social training or skills groups. One of the few empirical examinations of an outpatient social skills group with high-functioning children with autism (Barry, Klinger, Lee, Palardy, Gilmore, & Bodin, 2003) reports somewhat disappointing results. The children with autism in their study showed significant gains in greetings, spontaneous conversation, and play skills while interacting with typical peers who were trained to interact with children with autism. However, parental reports showed that outside of this controlled environment, there was virtually no carry-over effect. In nonclinic settings, the children showed gains only in relation to spontaneous and appropriate greetings. Another study of children in a social skills group reported that they showed significant gains in recognizing facial expressions and in problem solving but success outside of the group was never assessed (Solomon *et al.*, 2004). Thus, one must question the generalizability of most group skill interventions. For example, if one child in a social skills group wins a game, rather than tantrum, the other child can learn to say, "Good game. I bet I'll beat you next time!" Unfortunately, this response would not be appropriate if the child who won the game is upset due to a related, physical injury that occurred during the game, if the other child is leaving the group and will not be seen again, or if the child with autism who lost the game played at a very poor level and could not possibly amass the skills to win the next time. Problems can also occur if the other children or adults do not respond in the same way as "rehearsed" in a session. Teaching such rote responses can provide a scaffold for emergent social skills, but the danger is that these scripts will become static, and even problematic, in more novel or rapidly changing situations.

Although social skills training appears to show promise, and it provides some cost savings for parents and school districts, care must be taken to carefully evaluate its effectiveness outside of a controlled setting. As with any type of group therapy, it also becomes critical to carefully select and match participants. Although not examined in the literature, one mother of a five-year-old girl with autism noted wryly during an interview, "My daughter has been in a few of these things, and I think these social [skills] groups are only as good as the therapists running them." Because there is no formal, standardized protocol, therapists can be encouraged to select activities that have established, empirical support for promoting theory of mind, executive function, etc. Therapists must be able to figure out what types of rewards or behaviors motivate the children in their group, and parents should be included at all stages of the intervention.

RELATIONSHIP DEVELOPMENT INTERVENTION: SEEKING GENERALIZABILITY AND APPRECIATION FOR SPONTANEITY

Consistent with these previous reports of success, Steven Gutstein (2000) employed social skills groups in his practice with children on the spectrum. He became concerned, however, when he arrived early to a session to find the boys in one group sitting silently in the waiting room, showing no interest in communicating or playing with one another. Stunned, Gutstein asked them why they weren't talking, and one boy responded that he didn't receive a token (a reward) for being social in the waiting room. In essence, traditional social skills training worked for his patients only when they were actively seeking, and getting, an external reward. Gutstein then sought to develop social skills training that was intrinsically rewarding, and generalizable across situations. He theorized that children with autism do not clock the thousands of hours that typical children do as they scan the faces of their parents and peers. He and Rachelle Sheely studied research in typical development in an attempt to guide older children with autism through the same developmental steps that they should have encountered as younger children. Rather than focusing on memorizing scripts and relationship "protocols," he wanted to teach children underlying skills, including nonverbal communication. As Gutstein and Sheely note, "relationship skills are wonderfully portable and generalizable from one person and setting to another. Anyone who learns to be a real good friend will almost certainly know how to be a good son, brother, father, teammate, husband, and co-worker. Relationship skills are almost all interchangeable" (Gutstein & Sheely, 2002, p. 23).

Gutstein and Sheely named their social skills program Relationship Development Intervention (RDI; 2002). A core tenet of the program is to use underlying, basic behavioral principles as a way to help children learn to spontaneously seek out and receive internal reinforcement when they engage in joint attention and social referencing. Children are also led through a series of exercises that expose them to constantly changing circumstances and reinforcement contingencies. Reinforcement remains high, and the activities are typically fast moving, in order to help children find some pleasure in variety and success in rapid processing. This is critical for most children suffering from autism, who tend to adhere to rigid routines. In other words, RDI attempts, over time, to teach children to actually enjoy and seek out spontaneous social interaction, rather than "suffer through it" via intense, cognitive processing.

RDI attempts to increase a child's motivation to experience activities with others. Gutstein emphasizes the need to improve episodic memory, in which an emotion (e.g., joy, happiness) is attached to an event. A trip to an amusement park provides a fitting example. When asked what he remembers, a typical child may respond, "I liked going on the log flume with you! ... The race cars were so cool! I beat you when we went over the bridge at the end ... I smashed you good at bumper cars." There is often an element of shared experience and strong emotion associated with the memory. For a child with autism, however, remarks about going to an amusement park or some other type of "special" activity typically include descriptive statements that are devoid of social overtones. Their comments may also focus on what typical children and adults would consider extraneous or insignificant details. For example, Davon, a five-year-old suffering from autism, responded, "Yeah! I liked driving the orange race car. It had black stripes on the side ... It was really noisy in the bathroom." Although Davon was clearly excited about his visit, there is no sense that his joy was associated with being with his parents and brother, or his interactions with them.

A large number of activities are used to promote spontaneous social interaction, tolerance for change, nonverbal communication, and episodic memory. However, Gutstein and colleagues recommend that parents and children become well versed with the program, seek assistance from a certified RDI consultant, and engage in a formal assessment. Parental education is critical because parents function as the primary therapists. Formal treatment, or "lab time," is recommended for approximately a few hours per week, and various activities are to be dispersed throughout the day (i.e., the RDI "lifestyle") to promote generalization of skills. It is also important that children be accurately assessed so that activities are targeted appropriately to their skill level. Apparently, it is common that parents and therapists initially think children are more advanced than they really are. Children can often learn to "pass" socially without truly using or having nonverbal communication skills, such as social referencing.

For example, in one type of RDI activity, a parent and child sit facing each other. The parent sends a toy car down a chute to the child when, and only when, the child gazes at the parent's face. (Different cars are sent down the chute each time.) Then the activity requires that the child must gaze directly at the parent's eyes in order to receive the car. In essence, the goal is to help a child associate eye contact with "fun" and some appreciation for variety. Another carefully structured activity is for a parent to hide a desired toy under one of three large bean bags, and to have the child learn to follow the parent or coach's eyes to figure out which bean bag hides the "prize." In yet another RDI activity, children are asked to play the "silent game," in which they cannot talk, but only gesture, in order to communicate. In this game, children are forced to attend to nonverbal cues, but within the context of an enjoyable, reinforcing activity.

There are significant areas of controversy in RDI and other forms of social skills training. For example, in contrast to recommendations from many behavioral experts, basic tenets of RDI include *not* telling a child "look at me when I'm talking." This direct instruction is avoided in order to promote more natural learning that is not based upon or linked specifically to artificially occurring cues in the environment. The RDI protocol also suggests that children should avoid social interactions with peers until they are better prepared to interact and enjoy them. One-on-one time with a parent is recommended, particularly early on in treatment. And, when children begin to play with others, they are meant to be carefully matched with a peer of similar ability. According to RDI, typical peers or helpful "buddies" can actually prevent a child with autism from progressing socially because the typical peer will alter his own behavior to accommodate that of the child suffering from autism. However, some research suggests that children with autism who are able to imitate may acquire valuable skills and habits from interacting with neurotypical peers (Charlop, Schreibman, & Tyron, 1983). Other concerns about RDI may include its relatively high cost. Trained consultants are often in limited supply, and formal parent training can cost thousands of dollars. At time of writing, RDI is not well accepted or integrated into many school-based settings.

Although significant ambiguity exists regarding the effectiveness of social skills training, including RDI, it remains one of the most important areas for intervention. With social competence serving as one of the most significant predictors of success in life, clinicians must work carefully and consistently to address this critical, core deficit. As one four-year-old boy's mother stated, "All I want is for someone to call Ben for a play date. If he had at least one friend, I think things would be so much better." Clinicians can also work in interdisciplinary settings to encourage social group interventions with a variety of professionals and to help train teachers and caregivers to foster and model spontaneous social interactions. Even minor improvements in attention sharing and experience sharing can lead to significant benefits.

Chapter 7

The psychobiology of autism: coping with dietary restrictions, invasive procedures, and chronic pain

> After we treated Dylan's colitis, it's like he was a different child. He gained weight and started talking and playing more. And, he's doing so much better in therapy. No wonder he screamed and tantrummed so much before. I guess it's hard to do a lot of things when you are in so much pain.
>
> – Dylan's mother

A wealth of evidence is mounting that autism, like schizophrenia and bipolar disorder, has a biomedical component. Estimates suggest that up to 50 percent of children with autism suffer from painful, often untreated colitis, chronic constipation (Melmed, Schneider, Fabes, Philips, & Reichelt, 2000) or diarrhea, as well as various allergies and ear and yeast infections (McCandless, 2003). One recent study suggests that approximately 50 percent of the children with autism in their community-based sample, compared to fewer than 1 in 4 of the child control patients *admitted to emergency rooms* for abdominal pain, suffered from moderate to severe constipation. The children with autism also experienced significant discomfort due to fecal "loading" or impaction and distention of the large intestine (Afzal *et al.*, 2003).

Thus, one goal of this text is to help practitioners recognize that to ignore or discount the complex interplay between psychological and biomedical problems amounts to unethical behavior. For example, much as an increase in problem behavior among institutionalized elderly adults can be traced back to an inability to communicate effectively about untreated, severe pain (Camp, Cohen-Mansfield, & Capezuti, 2002), mounting evidence suggests that many problem behaviors observed among children with autism (e.g., tantrums, self-injurious behavior, refusal to toilet, disrupted sleep cycles; Afzal *et al.*, 2003) can be linked to similar difficulties with underlying, chronic pain and an inability to communicate. It is also important that therapists become familiar with some of the medical problems that children with autism typically possess. Deemed well beyond the scope of this text, parents can discuss the use of additional biomedical treatments for autism, including nutritional supplements (e.g., methyl-B12, magnesium, zinc), digestive enzymes, and chelation therapy (e.g., Edelson & Rimland, 2003; McCandless, 2003), with their specialty healthcare provider. Finding appropriate avenues for diagnosis and treatment is fundamental in order for subsequent, psychologically based treatments to achieve some measure of success. In other words, even the best therapist with the best technique is going to have only limited success when working with a patient in significant, physical distress.

Another unfortunate aspect of autism is that many children must have specific diets, either as a result of food allergies or an inability to process various proteins. Many children with autism have problems eating a variety of foods, for unknown reasons. Still other children suffer from significant metabolic and immune system dysfunction (Edelson & Rimland, 2003). As a result, children suffering from autism may be asked to undergo medical procedures such as blood draws, EEGs, and colonoscopies. Understanding how pain and discomfort can be managed better for these children is critical. Again, although this text is not meant to provide medical advice, mental health practitioners can use this information as a guide to help their patients converse better with medical providers to make such procedures go as quickly and smoothly as possible.

The most important thing that a mental health practitioner can do is to empower parents to communicate better with their physician, the individual performing the procedure, and their child. Sometimes parents may not initially feel that they can be assertive with their child's physician or lab technician. The argument "this is just a little pin prick and it's over and they will forget it; what's the big deal" is simply not acceptable. Pain clearly has a sensory and emotional component (Fernandez & Turk, 1992). Ignoring the emotional component can significantly heighten a child's perception of pain. Unfortunately, although a wealth of information is available regarding effective pain management techniques with children, most healthcare professionals remain unaware of them (MacLaren & Cohen, 2005). Children with autism cannot advocate for themselves. Empowering parents so that they can ask for, and even demand, appropriate, caring treatment for their children is essential.

CHRONIC PAIN AND UNDERLYING GASTROINTESTINAL PROBLEMS

Because many children suffering from autism are nonverbal, it is quite challenging to assess their physical state, including perceptions of pain. It becomes difficult to determine whether tantrums and refusing to toilet are related to problems with cognition, general frustration, or underlying medical conditions. Discerning whether a child suffering from autism is in severe or chronic pain is vital. GI distress, including constipation, diarrhea, and colitis, appears to present itself in approximately 50 percent of all children diagnosed with autism (Melmed, Schneider, Fabes, Phillips, & Reichelt, 2000). Special care can be given to observing children carefully both before and after going to the bathroom. The fecal matter produced by children with colitis or other GI problems can also be quite large, and it is often unusual in texture. Large amounts of mucus may be present. Despite these more obvious indicators, sometimes therapists can help parents communicate more assertively with their child's medical provider if they have concerns about underlying GI distress.

Some parents must become insistent and creative in order to get medical professionals to heed their concerns and provide additional assessment. For example, one father of a four-year-old son with colitis expressed significant frustration that their pediatrician said, "You know, all kids get constipated and all kids get diarrhea. I wouldn't worry about it." After a few visits with this kind of response and a helpful session with his individual psychotherapist, the father took one of his child's soiled diapers and placed it in a plastic bag to show the physician exactly what kind of diarrhea he was talking about. The father explained, "When [the pediatrician] opened that bag, I couldn't help but notice the look of shock on his face. He actually said to me, 'You mean that this is all from one accident?' I told him that he should finally believe me about how much fecal matter my son produced. I mean, it would often spill out of the diaper and run up his back or down his legs. The doctor finally relented and said, "Yes, this is not normal diarrhea." Additional diagnostic tests were then ordered, and their son was eventually diagnosed with colitis and treated successfully with medication.

Behavioral manifestations of pain, particularly among nonverbal children with GI distress, can often be observed and noted. Unusual posturing is common among children with constipation, diarrhea, and colitis (e.g., Afzal *et al.*, 2003). Many children will sleep on their stomachs, with their knees pulled up under them and their bottoms up in the air. One mother of a four-year-old boy with severe colitis noted, "I always thought it was just cute that he slept with his rump up in the air! I never knew that this was a piece of the puzzle." Still other children find that applying pressure to their abdomen, throughout the course of the day, provides some relief from the pain. A child who cannot speak may lean constantly against sofas and chairs, pressing his stomach against the sides, arms, or backs of the furniture, or spend a lot of time lying prone on the floor instead of playing. Another common posture associated with abdominal pain, particularly during a bowel movement, is for a child to lean forward or rock while sitting on the commode. Screaming and crying during a bowel movement is also common. And a child with little understanding of cause and effect may resist going to the bathroom, sometimes for days, in order to avoid the pain associated with a bowel movement. An unfortunate by-product of this coping strategy is severe constipation, which can lead to more pain during the next evacuation.

Such severe constipation can be linked, paradoxically, with accidents in which children soil their pants, often with diarrhea. Because the rectum and large intestine are so impacted and stretched, some fecal matter can leak out at inopportune times (cf., Afzal *et al.*, 2003). The good news about these GI problems, however, is that once they are properly diagnosed and treated, many autistic-like symptoms, such as tantrumming, poor sleeping, and toileting problems diminish significantly, along with pain (Edelson & Rimland, 2003). Why is this information so important for mental health and other practitioners? Psychologically based treatments for autism, then, have a significantly greater chance of success.

SPECIAL DIETS AND FEEDING PROGRAMS

Although the reasons for employing various diets and dietary restrictions for children suffering from autism are a source of constant debate (e.g., Cunningham & Marcason, 2001), many families institute casein-free (i.e., CF; dairy free), gluten-free (i.e., GF; wheat free), additive-free, or low carbohydrate (i.e., specific carbohydrate; SC) diets for their children with some degree of success. For example, although the Quality Standards Subcommittee of the American Academy of Neurology and the Child Neurology Society posits that there is not enough justification to support additional testing for the use of a gluten-free/casein-free diet (Filipek *et al.*, 2000), the only clinically significant predictor of moderate to severe constipation among children suffering from autism in a recent empirical study was milk (i.e., casein) consumption (Afzal *et al.*, 2003). Many individual reports suggest that GF/CF diets allow some children to think more clearly and concentrate better (e.g., Jackson, 2001). In other words, such diets may be useful on a case-by-case basis. Although the rationale for employing any of the aforementioned diets or interpreting allergy food test results is well beyond the scope of this book, advice can be given to help parents cope with such diets, if they choose them.

A first step for parents who employ any elimination diet (e.g., GF/CF, SC) is often to contact other parents or a support group. Various internet groups exist to provide a network with other parents, and many books are available either in book stores or through the internet. Aside from concrete suggestions about where to purchase pre-made pizza crusts without gluten and which brands are least likely to contain food additives, clinical psychologists and other mental health providers can help parents work through common feelings of anger and frustration regarding the difficulties inherent in implementing these diets. As noted by one mother, "We found a big difference when we removed artificial food coloring and preservatives from Brendan's diet … But, what a pain in the ass. I am so mad that I have to spend so much time each day making sure he gets the right food. I mean, I'm happy he's not tantrumming so much, but it's still a big giant pain."

Acknowledging the often unstated link between food and comfort is important. Helping parents grieve over such a loss (e.g., "I can't believe I can't even let my child enjoy a tootsie-pop because it has milk in it") can be a significant challenge if they wish to faithfully institute dietary changes. Many times a therapist can help parents acknowledge they are upset and angry, particularly in relation to how the circumstances affect their child and the rest of the family. One father stated, "My mother always makes these great Sunday dinners. And, it's like, how much time do we spend convincing her to make special food for Lisa, or to bring food over just for her. Then she doesn't understand why she can't eat what everyone else is eating. It just sucks. What could be a great family meal often turns into a nightmare." As with most other physical problems, examining the underlying family issues, particularly in relation to feelings of power, competition, and control becomes advisable. In this family, the father had a particularly difficult time expressing dissent with his mother for fear that she would remove her affection and emotional support, as well as her instrumental offering of food. When the father explained his reasons for adhering to his daughter's diet and showed his mother (the child's grandmother) various allergy and immune function test reports, she assented and began to make a few dishes each week that everyone in the family could eat and enjoy.

For other children, it becomes a chore to get them to eat much of anything, whether or not there is a formal diet in place. For example, it is not uncommon for many children with autism to have highly restricted, self-selected diets (McCandless, 2003; Prince-Hughes, 2002). For some families, this problem is a simple annoyance (e.g., "It's tough going out to eat; I can hardly find anything on the menu"), whereas for others it represents serious difficulties in lifestyle and in the child's health (e.g., "Brock just won't eat anything except crackers and milk – no vegetables. And, he's only in the 10th percentile for his weight.") For any parent, getting a child to eat a varied diet can be taxing, but it can be extremely stressful if the child tantrums severely, acts aggressively to self or other, spits out or vomits food, or has a dangerously low body weight.

Sometimes the rigid eating choices of children on the spectrum can be explained by aversion to various textures. Some children refuse to eat "crunchy" foods and select only foods with smooth textures. Other children with autism will not eat certain foods because they don't want to touch them, much less experience the feel of them in their mouth. One adult woman was misdiagnosed with anorexia nervosa as a child and adolescent; her aversion to texture was so severe that she would not even drink orange juice if it had pulp. "The color ... and texture ... of the foods I eat have always been more important issues than taste" (Anonymous, 2002, p. 44). She also reported that as an adult, she will "make [an occasional] concession to nutrition and eat a jar of baby food vegetables" (p. 48). For a while she experimented with pureeing vegetables herself, but found that even touching the raw vegetables became too averse. Unfortunately, she never received treatment, such as systematic desensitization and positive reinforcement for trying other foods, so her aversions to texture remain severe. Her diet continues to be limited, and her inability to eat typical meals in social settings also prevents her from engaging in a variety of everyday activities.

Therapists should be attuned to such problems to prevent lifelong eating disorders and malnutrition, as well as the related social problems associated with severely limited diets. Many hospitals and specialty centers, including Hershey Medical Center and the Kennedy Kreiger Institute at Johns Hopkins University, among others, now offer specialized feeding programs with a significant degree of success. Behavioral principles are used to introduce children to a variety of foods, with various textures, and suggestions are made to help parents cope with challenging meal-time rituals and restrictions. Sometimes a child responds well to simple reinforcement (i.e., time to play with a favored toy; a small piece of candy or bite of favored food) to trying a newly introduced food.

Depending on the severity of the child's symptoms and rigidity of eating routines, other feeding programs are more stringent and require timed food introductions, carefully controlled settings, and caloric monitoring. Some children must be desensitized to certain textures; others need help getting hypotonic throat and neck muscles strengthened to properly chew and swallow food. Because these programs can lead to dangerous outcomes if not performed and monitored properly, in which children refuse to eat or reject an even greater variety of foods, generalists must be careful to advise parents to engage in such intervention only under the care of trained professionals, such as behavioral specialists, nutritionists or occupational therapists. This is not a program that mental health providers should "try out" with their own clients without receiving considerable training and supervisory support.

PREPARING FOR BLOOD DRAWS, DENTAL WORK, AND OTHER INVASIVE PROCEDURES

Still another unfortunate, common experience for children with autism and their families is the need for a significant number of medical procedures. Many patients require blood draws, injections, colonoscopies or other invasive procedures. (Going to the dentist for filling a cavity, or even for a routine cleaning, can be stressful.) If families are not well prepared, the experience is typically traumatic for both the child and parents. One parent, Bob, remarked, "It wouldn't be so bad if [my four-year-old son] Pat didn't have to get that damn blood test [for liver function] every month. That throws us all off for about a week. We all hate to go and the lab tech hates to see us coming. The one woman who took Pat's blood was such an asshole. She actually told him, 'Stop acting like such a big baby. You're too old to be blubbering like this.' It's like she blames him for screaming and fighting, when he doesn't even understand what's going on. I just hate it that we have to do this to him, and no one can tell us anything to try to make it better."

For typical children, particularly nonverbal, preschool-age children, invasive medical procedures are often perceived as punishment and represent a significant source of anxiety and confusion (McGrath & Unruh, 1988). Children also do not develop a tolerance for repeated medical procedures. Without intervention, their level of anxiety remains consistently high (Katz, Kellerman, & Siegal, 1980). Some of the most problematic aspects of medical procedures include a change in routine, separation from parents, and physical restraint (Kuttner, 1989). Although a decision must be made on a case-by-case basis, sedatives can sometimes promote a feeling of helplessness during a painful procedure, or even have the unintended, unexpected result of exciting the child (Patterson & Klopovich, 1987). Thus, coping with medical procedures becomes even more critical for children suffering from autism.

Fortunately, based upon a collection of research in pain management, systematic desensitization, and behavior therapy, specific suggestions can be offered to help parents and children prepare for and cope with such medical procedures. Detailed suggestions can be offered to help parents and children prepare for blood draws especially. Please see Table 7.1 for a summary. Although the following discussion is limited specifically to that of undergoing blood draws, most of the general guidelines (e.g., discuss the procedure with lab technicians, doctors or nurses ahead of time; provide distractions and counterpressure) are relevant for any invasive procedure.

The following section provides very specific suggestions that therapists can offer parents and caregivers during a specific procedure, that of a blood draw. A detailed, extensive procedure is articulated here for two reasons. First, critical research indicates that the vast majority of healthcare providers, including those who work with children, are virtually unaware of pain reduction techniques (MacLaren & Cohen, 2005). And, second, this lengthy instructional section is included to help therapists empathize better with the experience of parents and their child with autism. The level of attention, detail, and constant demands for distraction and reinforcement can be overwhelming, and with such awareness therapists are better equipped to provide essential support.

Many parents experience significant anxiety when their child is asked to undergo a medical procedure, including that of drawing blood (Alderfer, Kazak, Cnaan, & Annunziato, 2005). For typical children, repetitive blood draws are perceived as one of the worst experiences encountered in medical treatment (Eland, 1985). But for a child suffering from autism, who may not be able to express himself verbally or who tantrums often, the experience can be even more traumatic for everyone involved. One critical element in making the experience as painless as possible for the child is to communicate with the staff at the laboratory well ahead of time and inquire about their general layout and procedures. In essence, parents should not expect to simply "show up" at the lab and find everyone there equally prepared. It often pays for a parent

Table 7.1 Guidelines to prepare caregivers for blood samples

1. Call the lab ahead of time for details
2. Prepare a Social Story
3. Do not lie to the child or provide false information (e.g., "Oh, it won't hurt at all")
4. Obtain an anesthetic cream (i.e., EMLA) if possible
5. Hydrate the child ahead of time if permitted
6. Double check arrival times at the lab with appropriate lab technicians
7. Complete paperwork ahead of time if possible
8. Arrive with two or three additional helpers
9. Shield the needle site from the child's view
10. Use proper technique for stabilizing the arm
11. Provide interesting distractions and counterpressure
12. Reinforce the child throughout the procedure ("You're doing great")
13. Apply appropriate aftercare, including pressure on needle site
14. Reward the child after the procedure

to visit the lab ahead of time and ask which phlebotomist "specializes" in children, and then arrange the appointment around this professional's schedule. Asking other parents about their child's experience with certain laboratories and technicians can also be helpful.

It also is important to find out how the laboratory is physically arranged, and to secure a setting in which a child can occupy an individual treatment room (with additional helpers) for the procedure, rather than endure it in the middle of a large room with multiple patients. It is important to confirm that additional helpers are allowed access to the treatment room. It helps to find out if a specific appointment time can be made, to avoid long waiting periods or to find out when things are particularly "slow." Some labs will even allot two technicians to a child when they are not especially busy. For example, one laboratory waiting room may be crowded at 6:30 a.m., when they open, whereas another lab across town may not typically become busy until 10:00 a.m. Yet other labs are busiest around lunch time or after 5:00 p.m. Thus, it is prudent to call and ask ahead of time and not make assumptions. It also can be well worth the extra effort to complete as much paperwork as possible before arrival. Some labs allow parents to FAX material in the morning or visit a day in advance to fill out forms. Calling ahead to confirm information is advisable. One mother called her lab ahead to confirm insurance information only to find out that her policy did not cover procedures performed at this specific lab. To avoid anxiety for all parties, every effort should be made to limit the time spent in the waiting room. If a child is particularly anxious, preparing a brief Social Story ahead of time can be helpful. (See Chapter 6 for an overview.)

Although this book is not meant to serve as medical advice, parents can always ask their physician to prescribe some kind of anesthetic cream to place on the child's arms. EMLA is a commonly prescribed version. Although the use of such a cream will not decrease the feeling that the child's arm is being held steady, or of the pressure from a tourniquet, it certainly deadens the area that receives the needle. The vast majority of parents who use such an anesthetic cream find that it significantly reduces pain and anxiety for their children. With such an anesthetic cream, however, additional suggestions can be offered to make its use more effective. (Of course, review and discuss all aspects of this medication with the child's physician.) For example, most people assume that the best sites for drawing blood are in the middle of the arm, at its crease. However, this is not always the case. Thus, the cream can be applied at the middle of the arm, at the crease, and above and below the crease. The cream can also be applied one inch to the left and right of the crease. It is also helpful to prepare both arms with cream. This way, the phlebotomist will have a number of sites to choose from. To keep the cream on the skin and not on a Band-Aid™ or gauze, the arm can be loosely wrapped with Saran Wrap™ or clingfilm several times and gently taped. Then a long-sleeved shirt can be worn to prevent the child from pulling at the tape. For some parents, telling their child that they are going to wrap the arm "like a present" or "like a big sandwich" sometimes helps with compliance.

With appropriate permission from the doctor who ordered the blood test, the child should be properly hydrated. It is surprising how much of a difference the amount of liquid consumed by a patient in the previous 12–24 hours can make to a phlebotomist. If properly hydrated, a child's veins appear more like small ropes than tiny threads. Thus, the child should drink plenty of water or some other noncaffeinated beverage well before the test. If the test needs to be done on an empty stomach, parents can double check with the prescribing physician to see if water is allowed. If fasting is required, perhaps overnight, scheduling the visit so that the child spends as little time without food as possible is recommended.

Two, or even three, additional helpers are advised in order to tend to the child when the parent is filling out paperwork before the procedure, as well as to provide helping hands and emotional support during the procedure. If a parent feels that she has no one readily available, she might be best advised to hire someone, a babysitter or paraprofessional, to come along. The cost for an hour or two would likely be outweighed by the benefits. Most parents who have employed these suggestions report that it is difficult to carry out the experience successfully without additional help.

When going to the lab, some accessories are also advised, such as a large beach towel or blanket, toys, books, or even a small DVD player or VHS camcorder. The towel will provide a visual barrier between the child and the phlebotomist, which may help to decrease anxiety and restlessness for the child. The toys and books provide other distractions and possible rewards. In the treatment room, immediately after the child sits down where instructed, a helper should be instructed to hold, or drape, the towel or blanket between the child and the phlebotomist *so that the child cannot see what the technician is doing.* This way, the phlebotomist can make several attempts if necessary, without the child knowing about each attempt. (This is not rare when working with children, who tend to have small veins, or if multiple vials of blood are required.) In many parents' experience, draping the area this way is one of the most fundamental parts of the procedure. Many times the parent may ask the child to sit on her lap, if this eases anxiety. It is generally helpful to ask the phlebotomist to keep the needles and tubes to be used behind this "curtain" and out of sight. Another helper should stand directly in front of the child with a book or DVD player to provide additional support and distraction. And verbal praise and reinforcement is recommended throughout the procedure.

It is important to remember that the anesthetic cream will not deaden the child's entire arm. He will feel his arm being held steady, and the pressure of the tourniquet. Healthcare providers and parents should not "lie" and tell a child that she will feel absolutely nothing. One mother would tell her son, "We are going to unwrap your arm [with the Saran Wrap™], and then the nurse [lab tech] is going to wrap it back up like another present. It won't hurt, but we will have to hold it still and press on it a little bit. You will feel some squeezing, but it shouldn't hurt." The gate control theory of pain (Melzack & Wall, 1965), at its most basic level, suggests that "biting the bullet" or applying pressure (counterpressure) or stimulation to another part of the body can diminish overall perceptions of pain. Sometimes gently rubbing or massaging the child's other arm or back provides such recommended counterpressure, as well as an additional distraction.

Holding the child's arm properly during the blood draw is important. Drawing blood from children, who tend to have smaller veins, is not always an easy task, and holding the arm still is essential. The person holding the child in his lap, with permission from the lab technician, can be advised to hold the child's arm at the elbow, to keep it from making any "up or down" motion. With the other hand, he can make an *overhand* grip over the child's wrist to prevent any rolling or "side to side" motion. An overhand, versus underhand, grip is essential. (With luck, the lab may have an additional phlebotomist perform this role, but sometimes only one technician is available.) It is important to hold the arm firmly, but not so tightly that it causes discomfort or pain.

Another critical part of the procedure occurs essentially after it is over. When the phlebotomist says, "I've got it!" or "I'm finished!" the tendency is to pick up one's child and run out of the lab. However, to prevent painful bruising or blue and yellow discolorations that may last for days, applying moderate pressure on the injection site for a full five minutes is necessary. Although some phlebotomists cause tissue damage, most have good technique. The problem remains that the blood clot that forms initially can move or shift if the child moves too much or too quickly after the procedure. If this clot moves (called "blowing the soft clot"), enough blood can back up under the skin to cause excessive bruising, hard spots, and painful pressure. Unfortunately, using a Band-Aid™ or even a "pressure Band-Aid™" is not sufficient to apply enough force to assure that a good clot has formed. An adult typically has to apply gentle but firm pressure with a thumb or finger. Thus, the child can be prepared ahead of time that she will have to sit quietly and watch some more video or read after the towel or blanket is removed. If possible, having the child "help" apply pressure (over a parent's hand) or having him keep track of the five-minute time period can help involve him and make this additional, but necessary, step more bearable. One resourceful parent even took a small kitchen timer along to help with this task. Finally, the child can be rewarded with a special activity, toy, or food.

Helping parents to become more assertive and to communicate better with their healthcare providers can also have significant benefits. Many phlebotomists appreciate the extra effort that parents take. One woman noted, "You know, sometimes I dread it when these little kids come in. They are always screaming and freaking out, and the parents don't know what's going on. Getting blood from a little kid isn't always easy, especially if their veins are extra small and they are squirming around. I wasn't so sure about this towel business, but I couldn't believe how well it went. It was like I could just focus on doing my job, as quickly as I could. The parents did the rest. It was great. I wish all of my patients did this, and sometimes I tell other people about the blanket and DVD player."

DENTAL PROCEDURES

Going to the dentist for a routine cleaning, much less an invasive procedure such as filling a cavity or extracting a tooth, can serve as a significant source of stress and anxiety for both parents and children on the spectrum. Empirical findings suggest that children suffering from autism are significantly more likely to associate fear and anxiety with going to the dentist than neurotypical peers (Matson & Love, 1990). This is not surprising when one considers the sensory disturbances and sensitivities often experienced by children on the spectrum, coupled with common difficulties with communication and transitions (Volkmar & Wiesner, 2004). Areas of concern surrounding a visit to the dentist may include the unusual or loud noises associated with various pieces of equipment, sitting with one's mouth open for a prolonged period of time, unfamiliar or unpleasant smells and tastes, the perception of pressure or pain, very bright lighting, and the presence of a typically unfamiliar practitioner.

Although it is difficult to outline specific procedures for any one dental visit or procedure, several helpful guidelines can be offered. For example, a number of case studies suggest that systematic desensitization and modeling can lead to more successful outcomes (Luscre & Center, 1996). Finding a dentist who specializes in children with special needs, and who has a pleasant personality, is crucial. In some cases, sedatives in the dentist's office or general anesthesia in a hospital operating room may be preferable. Discussing all options with the dentist ahead of time, even weeks before the procedure, is requisite. It also can be helpful for parents to have their children accompany them to their own dental appointments to provide appropriate modeling.

The following, specific guidelines may be useful in helping a child on the spectrum successfully complete a dental procedure. (For some children, a routine exam may even become pleasant.) Parents can be advised to ask other parents and professionals for recommendations. Local support groups may be of assistance. Families should consider ahead of time whether any dental procedure can or should be broken up into separate visits, if necessary. Creating and using a Social Story ahead of time can be useful; a number of books are already available on the internet. If a child has problems with oral sensitivity or reflexes, clinicians can guide parents to consider preparatory work with an occupational therapist. With permission, bringing a familiar item such as a teddy bear or blanket or squeeze ball can help alleviate a child's anxiety. Another approach is to schedule a visit to the dentist's office ahead of time to allow the child to meet the practitioners, see the treatment room, sit in the dental chair, and see and hear some of the instruments. Parents can also be advised to avoid spending extended periods of time in the waiting room. Scheduling an appointment when the office first opens, or immediately after the lunch break, is recommended.

Another important recommendation is to explain to the child what will happen and why, in language that he can understand. Be sure to tell the child when and how he will be touched. Neither parents nor professionals should lie to the child. For example, a parent or clinician should never state things like "Oh, this won't hurt at all," "The dentist won't hurt you," or "We will be done in five minutes or less" if they simply are not true. Showing the child the instruments to be used ahead of time can help minimize his anticipatory anxiety. (Whenever possible, allow the child to handle or "feel" the instrument. For example, the polishing attachment can be placed against a child's hand to help him understand what sensation to expect in his mouth.) Parents and professionals should also allow and encourage children to ask questions. Although having a parent or caregiver to sit next to the child, holding his hand, is also advised, in some cases, having a parent sit outside the treatment area, instead, may afford the dental practitioner more "authority." Clinicians can also encourage dental practitioners and parents to make short, direct statements in a calm tone of voice.

Providing verbal praise throughout a dental procedure, particularly when the child follows instructions or engages in appropriate behavior, encourages cooperation and minimizes stress among all parties involved. For some children, applying "counterpressure" by rubbing or patting an arm or leg during periods of anxiety or discomfort can provide a helpful distraction. Another simple but effective suggestion is to not position bright examination lights directly into the child's eyes. For both verbal and nonverbal children, involving them in the procedure whenever possible can increase their sense of control and cooperation. For example, a dental practitioner may be encouraged to tell a child, "Raise your hand if this hurts," "Show me which tooth hurts," or "Show me how you brush your teeth." Even encouraging a child to select a flavor of toothpaste offers an additional sense of control over certain aspects of the procedure. Parents should be advised to set up a clear reinforcement contingency in which the child receives a self-selected reward (e.g., a favorite treat or activity) at the end of the procedure. In addition, family members should expect that after any dental procedure, especially those including Novocain or sedatives, the child may wish to return home to a familiar environment with caregivers rather than return to school or day care. Becoming well-informed about aftercare instructions, in order to prevent complications and an unexpected, return trip to the dentist's office, is essential.

Additional considerations for invasive procedures include alternative techniques for distraction and forms of counterpressure. For infants and very young toddlers, rapid rocking can be quite effective in soothing a child and regulating his respiration. Rapid rocking means rocking the young child at a rhythm of 57 beats per minute. Slower rocking does not deliver the same benefit (Eliott, Fisher, & Ames, 1988). Having a parent present is also associated with a significant reduction in stress. Other forms of "counterpressure" include rapid patting on the lower back, along with the application of ice or gentle heat near the site of the procedure. Involving the child himself in coping directly, if possible, produces even better outcomes. Having a young child suck on a pacifier, or an older child blow bubbles or read a colorful or "pop-up" book, provides other excellent distractions (Kuttner, 1989). A child-centered approach assumed by all parties involved promotes the greatest benefit.

Chapter 8

Autism and academics: getting the appropriate education and IEP

There is often significant variation between a child's DSM diagnosis and the appropriate "educational classification" needed to guarantee services for that child.

The public school system in the US, including state-supported early intervention programs, can benefit children suffering from autism. However, obtaining appropriate services in a timely manner can represent a significant challenge. Mental health providers can assist families throughout the process of entering school in a variety of ways. Many can serve as advocates and sources of information to parents about basic issues of diagnosis and testing. This chapter will review and critique some general assessment instruments for autism and other developmental disorders, as well as offer suggestions for additional testing that may or may not be initially provided by public schools or early intervention programs. Concrete suggestions will be made for helping parents groom teachers for implementing various behavioral interventions, and to foster good relationships and open communication with school administrators. A discussion of the pros and cons involved in public versus private education will be provided as well.

INDIVIDUALIZED EDUCATION PLAN

All children receiving school-based intervention services need an Individualized Education Plan (IEP). Obtaining the right IEP is crucial for children and their families. Children typically spend a significant part of their day in a school environment, and for families with limited financial resources, these "free" educational services and interventions may be essential. Every single child is entitled to appropriate educational services regardless of family income, but for those with severely limited opportunities to gain outside assistance, or for those with language or cultural barriers, special help is sometimes necessary to guarantee access to publicly provided services. In many states, IEPs begin in early intervention programs, sometimes as early as birth to three years of age or three to five years of age. Thus, it is never too early to help families become familiar with the process and empower them to receive the best IEPs possible for their children.

EMPOWERING FAMILIES

Developing an appropriate IEP often presents significant emotional challenges for family members. Although one would certainly want to believe that school systems have the best interests of children at heart, the process is complicated by sometimes severely limited budgets, strict rules and regulations, and the impact of sometimes well-meaning but clinically uninformed administrators, school psychologists, teachers, and guidance counselors. For example, there is no guarantee that just because someone is a school psychologist, she is familiar with autism and its wide variations in symptom presentation, as well as recent updates in clinical research and practice. In some instances, parents, advocates, and generalist practitioners may have greater knowledge or familiarity. Therapists can help empower families to more successfully complete this process.

It is often important to offer practical guidelines to families as they negotiate the IEP process. Some broadly accepted suggestions include never signing anything at a meeting and always taking the materials home to "think things over." Just as someone rarely buys the first car they test drive, it is not advisable to assent to a child's evaluation or IEP during an initial meeting or review. It also is important that families know that they are entitled to bring anyone whom they wish to school-based meetings. For example, families can enlist the help and support and presence of friends, other family members, advocates, behavioral specialists, occupational therapists, lawyers, teachers, etc.

Another critical point is to help parents focus the meetings on their child. Based on basic social psychological principles, someone who is well individuated typically receives a greater proportion of resources and attention than someone who is not (Solomon, Solomon, Arnone, Maur, Reda, & Rother, 1981). It is important to focus on the child's name, and use the child's name often. For example, some parents bring along a picture of their child and place it in full view of everyone during the meeting. One administrator actually stated after such a meeting in which the parents displayed a picture of their child, "It was kind of weird seeing [that child's] picture at the table, but it really made me focus on what we were there for when the meeting got long." In addition, it is helpful to remind parents that they can and should be referred to by their name or appropriate title in an IEP or other meeting. Whether it is done innocently or not, it is simply inappropriate for meetings to take place with Mr. S, the school teacher, Dr. R, the principal, Ms. P, the school psychologist, and "Mom" or "Dad." When one mother politely asked that she be referred to as "Mrs. G" during her son's IEP meeting, she reported later that the entire tenor of the meeting changed, and she believed that she "was taken more seriously."

A child should be permitted to attend his IEP meeting and participate as much or as little as the parents deem appropriate. For example, one eight-year-old boy chose to come to the beginning of his IEP meeting and read a prepared statement (e.g., "I find Mrs. B's math class very tough. My aide helps me when I don't understand some of the instructions the first time. I also wish the lights didn't buzz so much ... I really like Mr. R's social studies class. When I sit up front it helps me pay better attention.") After he finished his statement, he left. In an ideal situation, the older the child, the more he can participate in his own educational programming and begin to effectively advocate for himself (Shore, 2005). Of course, for a child who is four years old and nonverbal, the situation is quite different.

Another fundamental factor in any IEP preparation is to insure that cultural differences are recognized and addressed within the context of a school placement. Parents and children are entitled to an interpreter at all meetings, free of charge, if English is not their first language. It is the responsibility of the school district to find and hire an appropriately qualified translator. This includes an interpreter for sign language if the child or anyone in the family has a hearing impairment.

BASIC EXPECTATIONS AND GUIDELINES

Reviewing all relevant rules and regulations regarding school placement and IEPs is simply too large a task within the context of the present text. In addition, many rules, regulations, and statutes change frequently, and they typically vary by state. Case law often provides guidelines for additional consideration. Thus, this chapter is intended to provide general guidelines, practical suggestions, and some additional resources for generalist practitioners.

Certain guidelines can be viewed as the foundation for planning IEPs. Important regulations for generalist practitioners to familiarize themselves with include the Individuals with Disabilities Education Improvement Act of 2004, referred to commonly as IDEA, and article 504 of the Rehabilitation Act of 1973. These guidelines generally posit that all children are entitled to a free and appropriate education. Critical information about these federal guidelines can be found on the internet and through local school districts. Some key constructs within these guidelines include (1) having the child placed within the least restrictive environment, sometimes referred to as LRE; (2) expecting that the child make reasonable progress toward educational goals; and (3) employing research-based programs or interventions. The definition of "least restrictive environment" is hotly debated (Fields & Ogles, 2002; Taylor, 2004). However, the overarching principle suggests that to the maximum extent appropriate, children with disabilities should be educated with children without disabilities. It also suggests that for a two-year-old diagnosed with autism, the LRE would be a learning program in the child's own home instead of a 45-minute bus ride to an unfamiliar school-based center. Seeking reasonable progress toward educational goals is intended to hold the school district responsible for providing appropriate intervention and to show that every child can rise to her potential. In essence, if a child receives special education and does not make any meaningful progress in a year, there is something wrong with the intervention, not the child.

The push for using research-based interventions exists, in theory, to prevent school districts from engaging in bizarre or experimental learning activities, curricula, or practices that are not particularly helpful to children. However, school districts may also use these criteria to purposefully or inadvertently prevent a child from receiving a useful intervention. For example, one seven-year-old child suffering from autism received a year of music therapy in school, and showed demonstrable improvements in speech and social skills. When it came time for the child's IEP, the school district wanted to discontinue the music therapy because only limited empirical research was available to support its utility in treating autism. Fortunately, the child's advocate noted that there was significant research-based evidence regarding the effect of music therapy – on that specific child in that specific classroom. So, the school district was persuaded to continue the therapy.

It is important to note that public schools, unfortunately, are *not* required to provide "best practice" or the "best education" for any one student, regardless of her needs. Instead, schools are required to provide a "reasonable and appropriate education" through various state and local mandates. For example, although Lindamood-Bell learning centers argue that they provide expert intervention and results for many children suffering from autism via carefully documented experiments and reports in peer-reviewed journals (e.g., Kennedy & Bachman, 1993), school districts may argue that this program is too expensive and that it is not easily adapted for use with students in individual classrooms. Rather, a school may state that it will substitute a different, but similar, empirically validated curriculum (e.g., Navigating the Social World, McAffe, 2001) because it is more cost-effective; it can be used to train school personnel, and it will allow the child to stay in school for learning.

An additional consideration remains that these guidelines typically include more classes than reading, writing, and arithmetic. Children are entitled to "specials," like music, art, and gym, just as typical children are. In addition to basic academic skills, such as the three Rs, many states now acknowledge that children's educational goals include social skills. Children with autism also may be entitled to an "extended school year," in which learning and reinforcement of that learning can take place all year, including the summer months. Extended school-year programs can also help children who deal poorly with the transition between a highly structured school year and a typically unstructured three-month-long summer vacation.

PRIVATE OR PUBLIC SCHOOLING

A major consideration for parents is whether to send a child with autism to private or public school. In some locales, public schools are generally superior to private schools. In other areas, however, private schools are typically superior to public schools in terms of teacher qualifications, student–teacher ratios, extracurricular activities, and special education provisions. But in the vast majority of cases, private schools are *not* required by law to provide one-on-one aides, assistive technology, OT, physical therapy (PT), speech, or any special programming for children with special needs. Some other points for consideration regarding the choice between private and public schooling include tuition costs, as well as the funding and time constraints related to providing transportation to and from school. In addition, some states do not require teachers to hold the same qualifications and certifications as those hired in public schools. Such differences in preparation may manifest themselves as deficits in understanding issues related to special education, and autism in particular. Parents must also consider student-to-teacher ratios; private schools typically offer smaller classes and more opportunities for individualized help.

If they decide to seek private school placement, and the public school does not agree, parents may submit a unilateral statement of their decision, in writing, to the public school. Parents can also request that the school evaluate their child and help pay for the cost of tuition or provide other services (e.g., OT, PT, speech). This process can often be lengthy and complicated, and the use of an advocate is recommended. As with all other guidelines for educational placements, some schools require advance notice to engage in any such process. As of time of writing, for example, Pennsylvania public schools require receipt of a formal, written statement of unilateral placement (into a private school) from a parent or legal guardian at least ten business days before school starts in order to even consider an evaluation for possible tuition reimbursement.

ADVOCATES

One thing that a generalist practitioner can do to help a child with autism, in relation to educational planning and crafting an appropriate IEP, is to assist the family in identifying and selecting an appropriate advocate. Some local mental health offices provide advocates either free of charge or for a small hourly fee. Other parents choose to hire an advocate privately. Although there is no formal certification for an advocate, and no regulation from state to state, some general guidelines can be offered in making a selection.

One vital consideration is the individual's educational background; does she have training or experience in special education, behavioral consulting, school administration, psychology, or social work? Some advocates are lawyers and even past marketing representatives. It makes sense that an effective advocate has the appropriate professional training. Beneficial characteristics of an advocate include attending conferences, staying current with rapidly changing rules, regulations, and statutes, a good professional reputation, and a flexible schedule with reasonable fees.

Many parents find that unless they have the time and the typically large, requisite amounts of money to engage in due process (e.g., a lawsuit against the school district), the value of finding an assertive yet nonadversarial advocate cannot be underestimated. Although knowing how to file appropriate grievances is important, some advocates believe that in the many months it typically takes to file multiple complaints and enter into a lawsuit with the school, much less resolve it, a child has already lost vital ground because only limited services may be in place. Although some circumstances certainly warrant or necessitate a lawsuit, the negative relationships and animosity that typically surround such litigation may also, unfortunately, put the child at an unfair disadvantage for future negotiations (S. Mierhoff, personal communication, July 23, 2005). Even though school administrators and other personnel are supposed to be objective in their dealings with any family, some educational personnel may develop animosity or a personal grudge if a lawsuit is filed. Parents have to make choices about seeking legal action very carefully.

EVALUATIONS AND TESTING

A school is required to provide, free of charge, an appropriate evaluation for every child who may need special services. Of course, arguments can be made that some school districts do not have the time, money, or resources to engage in the best testing practices. For example, some school districts with limited budgets may inadvertently test children with only a few instruments, and the report may present general summary information rather than a detailed examination of scattered scores and individual subtests. If a parent does not agree with the results of the school's testing, or if they think another opinion is important, they can obtain an outside evaluation and bring it to an IEP meeting. In most cases, however, it is vital that such outside or private evaluations include information from a child's teachers or professional caregivers, whenever possible. If the private evaluation does not consider feedback from teachers or other school-based personnel, the school district will often regard such reports as incomplete or misrepresentative (S. Mierhoff, personal communication, July 23, 2005).

Evaluation reports conducted by school districts or by early intervention programs should typically include a number of specific components. All evaluations should include a direct observation of the child, interviews with the child and parents, and interviews with the child's teachers or day care provider. Facts also should be gathered regarding developmental history, including medical information. Separate testing may be conducted with a speech therapist or pathologist, occupational therapist, and physical therapist. Speech testing should include individual assessments of receptive and expressive vocabulary skills, receptive and expressive language skills, pragmatic language skills, problem solving and reasoning skills, and auditory processing skills.

A school psychologist should attempt to assess intellectual or cognitive functioning, and may use instruments like the Wechsler Preschool and Primary Scale of Intelligence – Revised to obtain measures of Verbal, Performance, and Full-Scale IQ. (It is absolutely essential that any such testing be interpreted with caution, particularly if a child has limited language and attentional skills, or significant anxiety.) Another test of intellectual function often used is the Woodcock Johnson III Test of Cognitive Abilities. The Woodcock Johnson III Tests of Achievement Norms are also often used to help assess a child's level of functioning in academic or classroom-based settings. Instruments that can provide insight into a child's social and emotional functioning, completed typically by both parents and teachers, include the Behavior Assessment System for Children (BASC), the Social Scales Rating System, and an ADHD rating scale. The Vineland Social-Emotional Early Childhood Scales can also be of use. The Childhood Autism Rating Scale (CARS), or a similar instrument, may be employed to articulate and identify various problem behaviors and help make differential diagnoses.

ESSENTIAL GUIDELINES FOR CLINICAL RECOMMENDATIONS

One of the most significant aspects of a child's evaluation or testing report is the recommendation section. The wording is critical. One word out of place, or the "wrong" word or phrase, may determine whether or not a school district is willing or even required to provide services. Probably the most important thing for clinicians to consider in the recommendations section is the use of strong, clear, specific language regarding the child's needs and what is necessary to provide a reasonable, appropriate education and related progress toward goals. Weak language must be avoided. Please see Table 8.1 for specific examples. One phrase to *avoid* is "best practice." For example, a testing report should never include statements such as "the best practice for X is" or "the best approach to take regarding X is …." As noted previously, school districts are not required to provide the best or most optimal education, only a "reasonable and appropriate" education.

In contrast, the appearance of certain phrases in a testing report can demand appropriate consideration and garner critical attention from a

Table 8.1 Test report recommendations

Category	Specific language [the child ...]
Strong, compelling	requires X to receive an appropriate education needs X to make meaningful progress ... needs X, an appropriate, evidence-based treatment must have ... must avoid ... has an essential need for ... has issues that require ... will learn only under the following conditions ... will learn only when the following situations are addressed ... will only learn if ... will only benefit from ...
Weak, to avoid	would benefit from ... would be helped by ... would do well if ... would probably learn best if ... would learn better if ... should benefit from ... could be helped if ... may improve with ...
Inappropriate*	needs X, the most effective treatment available is entitled to X, the best treatment available demands cutting-edge treatment requires X for the best care needs X for the best education deserves above-average treatment

Note: * School districts are not required to provide the "best" treatment, only an appropriate educational experience. Ironically, language that indicates or even suggests that a specific treatment exceeds average or typical standards of care may give a school district justification to deny that recommendation, even though that specific treatment or intervention may be in the best interest of the child.

school district. Strong, unequivocal language must be used (see Table 8.1 for specific examples). A statement indicating that a child must avoid transitions in order to learn appropriately can help serve as justification for a specific, least-restrictive environment or an extended school year as well. The recommendations section is also the appropriate location to specify or justify requisite interventions or programs. For example, a statement could be made that a child needs a small class size, minimum student–teacher ratio, one-on-one aide, specials (e.g., music therapy;

art), recess (or a minimum amount of physical activity before academic work begins), occupational therapy, physical therapy, social skills training, peer support groups, assistive technology, an interpreter, etc. One of the most important things a mental health professional can do for a child is clearly state appropriate, specific, unequivocal recommendations in a testing report.

STUMBLING BLOCKS

There are a significant number of potential problems in relation to planning the most effective IEP for any child. Some of these stumbling blocks may be encountered because school districts wish to avoid providing certain services. In most cases, however, they may be due to genuine misunderstandings or misinformation among professionals or parents and professionals. For example, the child's given clinical or DSM diagnosis may not necessarily entitle him to appropriate services. As stated previously, in the state of Pennsylvania, schools are obliged to provide services for children diagnosed with autism, but not Pervasive Developmental Disorder (PDD-NOS). Although this may represent an ethical challenge if the two diagnoses differ significantly, clinicians can find out what diagnoses "qualify" for mandatory service provision in specific states and school districts and choose accordingly.

Another problem often encountered in developing an IEP is related to the fact that a specific educational service should not be tied to a specific disability. In other words, a child with Down's syndrome could be entitled to participate in an autistic-support classroom if this provides an appropriate educational experience. And a child should not be automatically placed within an autistic-support classroom simply because she is diagnosed with autism. Some children on the spectrum may even qualify for "gifted" classes or instruction. For example, one child with autism who is hyperlexic may receive an "appropriate education" by being in an autistic-support classroom for a few hours a day to receive social skills training, then spending a few hours in a typical classroom with an aide, and then working with a reading specialist. The school services must be tailored to the child's actual needs and not simply provide a "cookie cutter" or generic program for the diagnosis.

In many cases, the school district may state something vitally important, such as a stipulation or regulation (e.g., a child is not eligible to receive services unless she shows a 25 percent deficit in any one area, such as speech and language development or "Our lawyer said we don't have to offer home-based ABA programs anymore"), without providing appropriate source documentation. Sometimes these statements may come from a school counselor or superintendent, or they fall under the dubious heading of "just how we do things here." Of course, this kind of inaccuracy may be unintentional, but if such statements are unfounded or inaccurate, the results can be devastating for a child in need. Families must be trained to request a written copy of any such statements and their source. For example, consider one six-year-old boy, Tommy, who was tested and manifested a 20 percent deficit or delay in fine motor skills. His hand muscles were not well developed; his motor planning was poor, and he experienced severe pain if forced to write for long periods of time. The school district simply stated that he did not qualify for OT because his deficit did not meet the 25 percent cut-off. When Tommy's mother politely asked to see this ruling and its source in print, the superintendent replied, "Well, that's just what the rule is. I wish I could change it, but I can't." After politely repeating her request, the school agreed to provide documentation. After a few days, the school counselor called Tommy's mother and told her that they were mistaken. Apparently, the early intervention program in their state had a formal 25 percent cut-off in their written guidelines, but there was no such official cut-off for school-age children. Thus, Tommy qualified to receive OT services.

Related problems may occur if a school district feels burdened by the additional needs of other children, in large part due to the skyrocketing numbers of children diagnosed with autism. A school district representative may say, "We have so many more children in our district with special needs, now, that we simply can't provide all of these special services for everyone on our budget" or "We just don't have any openings right now in our autistic support classroom." These kinds of statements often lead to families feeling guilty, and thus requesting, or expecting, fewer services. Regardless of the expense and personnel issues involved, school districts are required by law to provide the most appropriate education for every child. One approach is to have a parent respond, "I understand that other children have needs, but right now we are talking about [this child]." Also, when a family or test report suggests a specific intervention or curriculum, some school districts respond, "Well, there is no need to put this in the IEP because it is just part of good teaching, and we do that all of the time, anyway." If a family hears such a remark, they should be counseled to counter such statements, and expect to present their child's formal needs and interventions in writing. A helpful response to such a comment is "Well, if [this intervention] is done automatically then it shouldn't be any problem to humor us and write it down in the IEP. I would like to see this in writing."

Another stumbling block can occur when a child with autism does not exhibit problem behaviors that garner much attention in a classroom. For example, a child who tantrums, yells, bites, screams, or does not sit still is recognized as having clear "problem behaviors" that require intervention. These kinds of behaviors are difficult for teachers and other children to ignore. However, many children suffering from autism engage in problem or stim behaviors that are not as noticeable or aversive to others, such as staring at lines and shadows, spinning their pencils over and over, flicking their fingers, staring into space, rocking back and forth in their chair quietly, and becoming catatonic-like and mute. These apparently unobtrusive behaviors may not disrupt a class, but they certainly make it problematic for learning and impair the child's ability to engage appropriately with other people and their environment. Unless an IEP specifically instructs teachers and other school personnel to look for and address these kinds of problem behaviors, a child will not learn. Special attention must be paid to these kinds of behaviors, and they must be targeted for intervention in writing.

Another problem often encountered is that many children on the spectrum present well during the school day but then exhibit major episodes of stimming, anxiety attacks, or violent behavior upon their return home. In essence, the children are able to monitor themselves and behave appropriately at school, but they do not have the internal resources to continue to do so once they come home. Stress and anxiety build up during the day, and it emerges in severe behavioral symptoms at home in the evening. Some signs of increasing stress during the school day may include finger sucking or chewing behaviors, heavy eraser marks and other perfectionist behaviors, balling up fists, or squeezing up against people or things (S. Mierhoff, personal communication, July 23, 2005). In these cases, extra attention from teachers to help modulate stress, or extra periods of recess, for example, may be useful. However, some school districts regard such evening outbursts as evidence that the child does not receive appropriate discipline from parents or that their problems are "emotional" due to problems at home. Families should be cautioned to help avoid and counter this line of thinking in order to receive appropriate services for their child during the school day.

Another common pitfall encountered by families is that school districts sometimes attempt to write into an IEP that they will slowly remove or titrate the frequency of services. For example, a school representative may say, "Danny is doing so well. Let's write down here that we will cut back his one-on-one aide from 5 hours a day to 3 hours a day in one month, and then down to one hour a day in two months." It is best for parents that the IEP include as many services as possible. Another IEP meeting can be called, at any time, to change things if the child is doing well and services need to be removed or cut back. It is generally much more difficult to convince the school to schedule another IEP and "replace" missing or titrated hours or services if the child regresses.

DOCUMENTATION FOR PROGRESS

Even the most well-constructed IEP is meaningless if it is not well executed. Children suffering from autism who have significant developmental delays cannot afford to "waste" a year without making progress. Documenting progress via empirical data is a vital step toward accomplishing real learning. It is not appropriate for a child to receive a "P" for passing or "E" for "emergent skill" in relation to a specific educational goal. Progress should be measured as specifically and empirically as possible. What does "emergent skill" really mean, anyway? Does it mean that the child engages in reciprocal communication? The best measurements are data-driven and can be distilled down into a number or series of numbers. A commonly employed goal is to observe a child's participation in a specific behavior or proficiency at a certain task 80 percent of the time. For example, to help assess attention, a child can be observed in three five-minute periods during a classroom session to measure the amount of time the child sits still and maintains eye contact with the teacher. This kind of observation produces a specific number or percentage that can be used to measure progress against previous results as well as a desired goal. Another benefit to this data-driven approach is that it helps operationalize certain learning goals and skills, and it assists teachers in both promoting and measuring progress. Aides can help with this process, as teachers are often overwhelmed or unable to keep such data. Providing a central notebook in the classroom or learning center for all data tracking is recommended.

IT IS ULTIMATELY ABOUT THE TEACHER

Still other potential problems include having to work with teachers who are less than understanding or educated about implementing appropriate behavioral plans in the classroom. Even with the best IEP, children have limited opportunities for success if their teachers are not involved and committed. One mother of a six-year-old boy with autism stated, "I really needed someone to help me educate Kieran's teacher. It's like this woman couldn't get it in her head that most kids with autism are *not* mentally retarded; they usually just have trouble expressing themselves. This teacher talked down to Kieran, like he was really stupid or something. I mean, Kieran can write his name, he knows all of his phonics, and he can count to 100!" Fortunately, the family's therapist helped Kieran's mother gather some articles to give to his teacher, and she worked with everyone involved to formulate a behavioral modification plan that the teacher could implement easily in the classroom.

Interestingly, one potential publisher for this current text demanded that only positive information about teachers be presented, and suggested that because teachers work very hard and are asked to take on more and more responsibility within their classrooms, there was no sense in criticizing them. Although the point is well taken, it is important to note that for many children and their parents, some teachers do engage in behaviors that are inappropriate or uninformed. To ignore these problems violates basic tenets of validating a patient's experience and advocating for children in general. To reiterate, the purpose of this chapter is not to denigrate teachers, but to help generalist practitioners help their patients and families work within a typically complicated and challenging system, which may include the sometimes inappropriate behavior of both experienced and inexperienced teachers.

Sometimes the best way to involve a teacher is to provide open avenues of communication. One parent found that by giving her child's teacher her cellphone number, with specific permission to call at any time of day, for any reason (e.g., to report a concern or to ask for help), the teacher's attitude improved significantly. Another approach is to supply the teacher with a notebook to comment in, which serves as a log that travels back and forth with the child to and from school. Knowing that the child's parent (and hopefully BSC, paraprofessionals, or other relevant support personnel) read and review the notes daily can provide additional teacher support. As one teacher noted, "I don't mind going out of my way to do things to help Marc … It just helps to know that someone notices." Yet another teacher explained, "As long as I know that it is OK to tell a parent that I'm having a hard time and getting frustrated, and they can handle it so that we can work it out, I'm much more prepared to go that extra mile." In essence, teachers need appropriate positive reinforcement, too. Although it may seem unfair to parents to have to provide so much additional emotional support to teachers and other school personnel, it is ultimately in the best interest of the child.

Another critical factor in constructing an IEP is to provide appropriate educational and supervisory support for all involved teachers and staff. For example, specific guidelines could be included in the IEP to provide a certain number of hours for one-on-one aides (i.e., paraprofessionals) or a more general teachers' aide in the classroom. Additional support can be included, such as in-service training for teachers and aides, or even financial support or incentives for teachers to attend conferences or workshops about autism. Some parents or advocates may even recommend that the IEP allow for school administrators and psychologists to receive additional training in autism. Formal provisions for teachers to receive regular supervision, perhaps with a well-trained school psychologist or BSC, can also be provided. In essence, in order for teachers to properly support a child, they could expect to receive the appropriate education and support themselves. A well-tailored IEP that sustains teachers, coupled with consistent parental involvement, can help make this possible.

TRANSITIONING TO SCHOOL

Transition to school can be extremely stressful for both children and their families, particularly when a child has difficulty coping with any transition or change in the daily routine. Some children who experience significant progress in ABA home-based programs regress severely when placed in a relatively crowded, public school setting. Early intervention services are not always seamlessly integrated with school-based services, and families must rehash IEPs, deal with transportation to a new school, and become familiar with new teachers and school personnel. Sometimes funding streams change, and families must seek out information and advocates to help their child to continue to receive additional services. One mother of a five-year-old with autism remarked, "This has been the worst year of our lives. I had no idea it would be like starting over. Now Josh hates school. When I went to observe him, he stood in the corner a lot of the time with his hands over his ears, or he sat in his chair and flapped. It was just awful to see. He was doing so well before!" Therapists must be aware of this potential danger and work proactively with families to ease the transition.

Some concrete suggestions can be offered to help children transition more effectively to a new school environment. One mother worked with an advocate and her BSC to help arrange a formal classroom visit for her child before the school year began. For a few hours, she and her son went to visit the school, walk the halls, go into the classroom, and even talk with his teachers. (This mother also brought a small gift basket to the school. Although this should certainly not be required to receive appropriate services, the mother felt it helped provide some essential positive reinforcement and goodwill.) Another child's IEP included a before-school visit, featuring a dry run on the school bus and some playtime on the school playground. Becoming familiar with the school environment in the absence of new children and ambient noise and activity can be beneficial.

Still other parents request permission to contact other children and their families who will be in the same class. Arranging a therapeutic play date before school starts, in a familiar environment such as their home or favored playground, can help significantly. Yet other schools offer, or families and advocates encourage the school to start, "buddy programs," in which children are paired up before or at the beginning of school for planned socialization or play. Due to its unstructured nature, recess can be a source of significant difficulty for many children with autism. One elementary school offered a recess "buddy program," in which certain children with autism were scheduled to play together with typical peers and a speech therapist to facilitate appropriate and enjoyable activities at recess. Buddy programs have been used within the context of regular classrooms and study halls, and empirical research suggests that such programs may have value (e.g., Laushey & Heflin, 2002).

One aspect of school-age transition typically overlooked is eating in the cafeteria. For many children with autism, the loud noises, bright colors, flurry of activity, new people, and even the presence of television (yes, this is common practice in some schools) can distract them from the vital task of eating. Children with eating problems may become overwhelmed with sensory input or become so distracted that they do not eat enough of their lunch to satisfy basic nutritional needs. Although it is difficult to control the auditory stimulation at lunch time, with so many children eating together and talking in one room, some concrete suggestions can be made that children with autism use utensils with a dull finish and plainly colored plastic or paper plates. Offering a reward when all foods are sampled or eaten can be helpful as well. Finally, playing or broadcasting music at a slower tempo (e.g., Mozart) can help slow down over-stimulated children's breathing and heart rates (Ernsperger & Stegen-Hansen, 2005). All students, as well as the teachers responsible for overseeing the lunch room, may benefit from such restful background music.

Chapter 9

Newer treatments, resiliency, and hope for the future

The goal of this chapter is to review research on innovative and adjunctive treatments for childhood autism, to promote resiliency among parents and family members, and to address additional sources of hope for the future. Emergent treatments include neurofeedback (NF), individual psychotherapy, and eclectic therapies, such as art, music, and pet therapy. Although these therapies do not enjoy the same mainstream support as ABA and other, more intensive, behavioral therapy programs, they may be employed carefully on a case-by-case basis. Additional information will be presented regarding coping and resiliency, including humor, spirituality, the untapped role of grandparents as a source of support, and general hope for the future.

Children suffering from autism appear to manifest a variety of neuropsychological differences in brain function. As noted in Chapter 2, recent studies suggest that children with autism do not have (or present with impaired functioning of) "mirror neurons" (i.e., a part of the brain that compels us to mimic or empathize with others) when compared to NT peers (Williams, Whiten, Suddendorf, & Perrett, in press). Another emergent area of study and intervention involves the differential brainwaves produced by children with autism. Although few controlled studies exist, there appears to be some promise that a modified form of biofeedback, known as neurofeedback (NF), can help some children learn to modulate their own brainwaves without the use of drugs or other psychoactive agents.

BRAINWAVE FREQUENCIES

The brain generates a variety of waves, which represent the rhythmic firing of neurons (for a detailed review, see Robbins, 2000). The four primary wavelengths are delta, theta, alpha, and beta waves. Delta waves are low-frequency waves, occurring between 1 and 3 hz for adults and 1 and 2 hz for children and teens. They occur primarily during stage 4 of deep sleep. If delta waves occur during a normal "waking" state, they are likely to indicate the presence of a coma, brain damage, or a severe learning disorder. Interestingly, delta waves are also present when the brain produces growth hormone during periods of deep sleep. Theta waves are also considered low frequency brainwaves. They occur between 4 and 7 hz for adults and 3 and 5 hz for children and adolescents. Theta waves are associated with hypnogogic states (a precursor or early stage of sleep in which it is difficult to tell whether one is awake or asleep) and intense periods of daydreaming. Memories may be available, but they are deeply internalized. In other words, this state is associated with "zoning out," and is not appropriate for active listening, reading, or learning. The presence of theta waves is also associated with seizure activity.

Alpha waves are higher-frequency brainwaves. They occur between 8 and 12 hz for adults and 5 and 7 hz for children and some teenagers. Clinical research suggests that higher-frequency alpha waves, those between 10 and 12 hz for adults and 6 and 7 hz for children, are associated with a very alert yet relaxed state. Examples of alpha wave activity include someone involved in meditation who is relaxed yet alert, someone musing over ideas to exercise their creativity, and a goalie poised in the net awaiting the opposing team to shoot a puck. The peak frequency of alpha is often associated with innate intelligence. Individuals suffering from diffuse brain damage or severe mental retardation rarely produce alpha waves, and if they do, these waves are usually in the lower-frequency range.

Beta waves are another type of higher-frequency wave. They occur between 12 and 18 hz in adults and 12 and 14 hz in children, and represent waking consciousness. Beta waves in the higher frequencies are associated with decreases in anxiety, decreases in impulsivity, active problem solving, and general alertness. If produced in the sensorimotor cortex, typically between 12 and 15 hz for adults, this type of beta wave activity is referred to as SMR (sensorimotor rhythm) and is associated with restful alertness, decreases in sensory overload, and an increased ability to tolerate painful stimuli. Brainwaves are also produced in higher frequencies, between 19 and 40 hz. These higher frequencies can be referred to as "high beta" waves and are unfortunately associated with anxiety and cognitive rumination. An appropriate analogy is a car revving in neutral; energy is expended for little or no benefit. These high beta frequencies have also been observed among individuals suffering from alcoholism and depression.

It is important to note that no one brainwave or frequency is good or bad in itself. All brain activity occurs within a situational context. The critical issue is whether a child or adult produces brainwaves that are appropriate and productive for a specific situation. For example, during a typical sleep cycle, at 2 a.m., it would be beneficial for a child to produce delta waves, whereas during a math test at school, it would be ideal if the child could produce a significantly greater proportion of beta waves. During an uncomfortable medical procedure, the generation of alpha or SMR frequencies would be helpful.

QEEG

Quantitative electroencephalography (QEEG) is a process that specially trained clinicians can use to assess overall brainwave activity. Asking a child with autism to undergo a QEEG can be quite challenging. An individual must sit still while a specially fitted cap with at least 30 individual electrodes is placed against the scalp with conductive paste, and then wires are attached to those electrodes via a computer. Patients are typically asked to sit quietly for a few minutes, first with their eyes open and then with their eyes closed. Sitting with eyes closed provides the best measure of alpha wave production. Having a child with autism sit still with his eyes open or closed while hooked up to an elaborate, gel-filled cap and tethered to a computer often proves one of the more difficult parts of the QEEG procedure. Some clinicians have found that reading a detailed Social Story at least a month ahead of time and "practicing" at home with a tight-fitting swim cap can help prepare the child for an actual QEEG (J. Bradstreet, personal communication, July 26, 2003). In more challenging situations, some clinicians conduct a modified QEEG with only a few electrodes to at least gather some baseline data regarding brainwave production. With the help of specialized computer programs, clinicians can assess whether an individual has more slow or fast wave activity in certain parts of the brain. A QEEG reading can also help clinicians determine whether the neuronal firing in the brain is synchronized across hemispheres or among different lobes. In other words, the brain may produce enough fast wave activity but remain out of synch across the brain, and, thus, not transmit information effectively (see Robbins, 2000, for a review).

Certain psychiatric disorders, such as Attention Deficit Hyperactivity Disorder (ADHD), appear to have recognizable QEEG patterns or signatures. For example, research suggests that QEEG readings can correctly identify 90 percent of individuals clinically diagnosed with ADHD, and that QEEG readings can correctly rule out ADHD as a diagnosis for 94 percent of those individuals not diagnosed with ADHD (Monastra, Lubar, & Linden, 2001). Various data sets also suggest that a preponderance of theta and delta waves, including overall cortical slowing in the frontal or parietal lobes, is consistent with a diagnosis of autism. Children suffering from autism also generate a significantly smaller proportion of alpha and beta waves by comparison (Thompson, 2002).

Lubar, Monastra, and colleagues (Lubar, 1995; Monastra, Lubar, Linden, VanDeusen, Green, Wing, Phillips, & Fenger, 1999) conducted various studies of children (aged 6–12) and adults who were categorized as neurotypical or given a diagnosis of ADHD or autism, and the types of brainwaves that they typically produce. The unit of measurement employed was the numeric ratio of theta to beta wave production, referred to as a "power ratio." In Lubar's study, this power ratio was 1.8 for NT children and 3.0 for adults. In contrast, adults suffering from ADHD had power ratios between 3.0 and 5.0, and children with ADHD displayed an average power ratio of 10.0. Thus, individuals with ADHD appear to generate significantly more theta than beta waves during periods of wakefulness.

In the final group, comprising adults and children suffering from autism, the results were even more profound. Both children and adults diagnosed with autism displayed a power ratio of 20 to 60; their brains generated 20 to 60 times more theta waves than beta waves during periods of what should be normal wakefulness. In essence, children and adults suffering from autism, compared to typical peers and even those suffering from ADHD, produce a preponderance of theta waves, associated with zoning out, hypnogogic states, and even seizure states while wide awake. Such information may make it easier for parents and teachers to understand the symptom presentations of children suffering from autism when they realize that an affected child may not necessarily be willfully ignoring them or the people around them. It also remains unclear why children suffering from autism tend to produce these low-frequency brainwaves. Fortunately, some children appear to respond well to an emergent therapy referred to as neurofeedback.

NEUROFEEDBACK TRAINING

Clinicians may employ neurofeedback (NF) therapy, a specialized type of electroencephalogram biofeedback, in an attempt to increase the ratio of fast wave to slow wave brain activity. Once an initial QEEG is conducted, or at least some baseline frequency data is gathered, treatment sessions may last between 10 minutes and 50 minutes. The length of the sessions often varies, depending upon the patient's age and the ability to sit and attend to various computer-generated NF programs. According to Lubar (1995) and Thompson (2002), children with autism may require more than 100 training sessions, whereas children suffering from ADHD may benefit significantly after 30 to 50 sessions. During an individual treatment session, baseline data are taken, and patients then progress through a series of individually tailored NF programs. By playing specially constructed "computer games" that respond directly to a patient's brainwave activity, as assessed by a series of electrodes, individuals learn to normalize their QEEG pattern. A common, desired outcome is a decrease in power ratio; theta waves are "trained down," while beta waves are "trained up."

For children with autism, astute practitioners tailor the computerized feedback to their particular interests. Feedback is provided immediately, in accordance with parameters set by the practicing clinician. For example, one program may display a car that morphs and "dances" when the ratio of fast to slow brainwaves increases. For another child, a Pac-Man™ type figure may venture through a maze when beta waves increase. Still another program plays favored music when theta wave production decreases below a preset limit. Just as in basic operant conditioning, a pleasant tone or song or interesting visual effect occurs when higher-frequency brainwaves are produced more often, and when lower-frequency brainwaves are inhibited.

How does a child with autism, who may not be able to speak, know how to alter his brainwaves? Although most children suffering from autism are unable to fully articulate their internal experience during NF, some children and adolescents with ADHD have described the experience as "learning to be more awake while sitting still," "letting my mind expand," or "letting my breathing fill me up to let my mind do its work." Every patient's experience appears to be different and difficult to describe. Typical adults who engage in NF have described learning to increase beta wave production "like learning to sit still, poised but ready to pounce, like a cat" or "like a basketball player, standing still but alert on the line." Still others equate beta wave production with the feeling experienced during meditation or even karate. As articulated by one NF practitioner, "neurofeedback helps people to be more attentive to being attentive" (Butnick, 2005, p. 622). Fortunately, individuals who practice NF, including children with autism, do not have to explain how they increase fast wave production; they can simply learn to do it. Explaining how to increase or inhibit a certain brainwave often proves more of a challenge than altering the brainwave activity.

Despite the ability of NF therapy to alter or adjust brainwave production, some experts caution that care must be taken to generalize training so that children learn to produce fast wave activity outside of a controlled, clinical setting. After initial success with various computer game-type programs, practitioners should encourage children to engage in NF therapy, producing the desired ratio of fast to slow wave activity, while engaged in otherwise "boring" or challenging tasks like reading and math homework (Thompson & Thompson, 1998).

Metacognition, learning to think about one's thinking, is a related, three-step process that can be enhanced in children with autism. In metacognition, a person or child must first identify what he is doing (e.g., subtracting numbers). Second, he must examine how he performs that task. For example, does he subtract by memory, on his fingers, or by "negative addition?" For the final step in the process, he must be able to analyze how well he performs at that task. In other words, does his particular method work, and why or why not? The child can consider, "Should I do the same thing, or something different next time, and why?" Clinicians can also help children create habits for producing appropriate higher-frequency brainwaves in different settings. For example, a child can practice first taking three deep breaths before engaging in NF training, and then taking those same three deep breaths in school before a spelling test in order to help promote those desirable higher-frequency brainwaves (Thompson & Thompson, 1998).

Empirical studies suggest that NF is an effective treatment for children and adults suffering from ADHD (Monastra, Lynn, Linden, Lubar, Gruzelier, & LaVaque, 2005). A benefit of NF appears to be the lasting effects on symptom reduction, typically without the use of psychotropic medication. Some studies indicate that if a child suffering from ADHD takes medication and then stops, her symptoms will return. However, studies also show that children with ADHD who receive NF maintain symptom reduction, even after treatment has been stopped for over a year (Lubar, 1995).

Although fewer empirical studies are available regarding the impact of NF upon the primary symptoms of autism, a number do indicate that NF can be useful in reducing some specific behavioral symptoms. For example, Jarusiewicz (2002) found that for 12 children suffering from autism receiving NF treatment, compared to 12 children matched for age, gender, and symptom severity in the control group, the majority showed significant improvement as measured by a treatment evaluation checklist and parental assessment. Specifically, children receiving NF were reported by parents to present with less anxiety, fewer tantrums, better sleep cycles, and increased socialization and vocalization. A number of case studies also suggest that NF can be useful in the treatment of childhood autism (e.g., Sichel, Fehmi, & Goldstein, 1995). One study found that children who participated in more than 100 treatment sessions demonstrated significant increases in IQ and academic performance (Thompson & Thompson, 2003). Other potential benefits of NF treatment include an opportunity to help children suffering from autism cope better with anxiety and stress, without the use of drugs or other psychotropic medications. With NF, virtually no side-effects have been reported. However, it is important to remember that if children are nonverbal, or have difficulty expressing themselves, it may be difficult to ascertain whether or not any less obvious side-effects occur. And until additional research is conducted with double-blind studies, the treatment may be considered experimental within this specific diagnostic category (Robbins, 2000).

Finding a qualified practitioner may be difficult for some families. Some practitioners may employ NF in their practice, but they may focus almost exclusively upon "high or peak performance" for athletes or executives, or upon treatment for seizure activity or ADHD. Few clinicians appear to specialize in the treatment of childhood autism. Although some clinical internships offer training in NF, many state boards do not offer formal licensure in biofeedback itself. One option is to find a licensed psychologist or healthcare provider who has completed a series of training courses or certification programs endorsed by various professional organizations. The cost of treatment may also be prohibitive. A QEEG, including interpretation, can cost as much as, or more than, $1,000, depending upon the clinic and practitioner. Individual sessions of NF may range in price from $50 to $150. Considering that children suffering from autism require many sessions of NF, the total cost of treatment may extend to thousands of dollars. To compound the problem further, many private insurance companies will not pay for NF or for a QEEG, particularly if the presenting problem is identified as autism.

Still other families have to travel a great distance to find a practitioner. One mother found that NF helped her son concentrate better, but she had to stop treatment because the three-hour, round-trip car ride began to prevent him from doing well in school, and the rising price of gas made their bi-weekly travel considerably expensive. In certain cases, either due to the travel required for treatment or for simple convenience, practitioners will allow patients to rent specially designed NF equipment for home use. In these instances, a parent or other caregiver receives initial training in delivering NF in the practitioner's office, and then takes the equipment home to initiate treatment. After a certain number of sessions, information regarding the child's progress is sent via computer or FAX to the practitioner for review. Treatment protocols are adjusted, and new instructions are given through formal or informal supervision, and NF continues. For some families, especially those in isolated geographic areas, this arrangement appears to work quite well. Children trained at home can typically receive more sessions more often, sometimes in a variety of settings. Of course, additional fees are incurred, typically between $300 and $400 a month for equipment rental alone. The question also remains how well any individual parent or other caregiver can be trained to accurately affix electrodes, assess electrical impedance, run the NF programs, adjust expected frequency thresholds, document and monitor a child's progress, and respond to clinical supervision. Some may do quite well; others may not. Children themselves may also dictate how well home-based NF is conducted. A compliant, more passive child may listen quite well to a parent's instruction, whereas a resistant child with significant problems with impulse control may not.

ADDITIONAL TREATMENT MODALITIES: MUSIC, PET AND ART THERAPIES

Additional therapeutic approaches have been adopted for use in the treatment of childhood autism, often as adjuncts alongside more mainstream therapies such as applied behavioral analysis. Some of these therapies, including pet, art, and music therapy, have been in existence for quite some time but have only been more recently employed with children suffering from autism. Therapists can be cautioned that pet and art therapy enjoy only limited empirical support in terms of controlled studies. However, other studies and case reports suggest that their use may be beneficial and typically free from any undue risks and side-effects. As demonstrated in a recent meta-analysis, music therapy shows considerable promise as a therapeutic technique (Whipple, 2004). Thus, the use of these various interventions in an overall treatment package can be explored as an adjunct to more mainstream, behavioral therapy.

A recent meta-analysis (Whipple, 2004) of nine empirical studies of music therapy as a treatment for autism suggests that this type of therapy demonstrates consistent, considerable benefits. All studies included in the meta-analysis employed a randomized, experimental design with children or adolescents who suffered from autism, and featured music therapy as a separate, independent variable along with a related, no-music-therapy control condition. An overall effect size of $d = 0.77$ was obtained, with a mean weighted correlation of $r = 0.36$, $p<0.01$. Confidence interval data and homogeneity values also indicated that all effect sizes were in the positive direction, indicating a clear benefit from the use of music therapy. Music therapy itself was defined to include a variety of techniques, including learning to play an instrument, singing or following rhythms with crude instruments, either alone or in small groups, and even listening to background music during academic or social tasks such as eating lunch. Music therapy, regardless of the active or passive form in which it takes place, appeared to help children suffering from autism improve their auditory discrimination skills, decrease the frequency of self-stimulatory behaviors, improve vocabulary comprehension, improve eye contact and spontaneous speech, and reduce meal-time "out of seat" behaviors (Whipple, 2004).

A two-year longitudinal study of music therapy interventions with children suffering from autism mirrors the range of such benefits and suggests that these positive outcomes generalize outside of specific music therapy sessions (Kaplan & Steele, 2005). Approximately half of the studies included in Whipple's meta-analysis were actually conducted by trained music therapists; the others were conducted by psychologists, occupational therapists, or special education teachers. Thus, music therapy in one of its various forms could be included, in a variety of settings, in a child's treatment program.

In pet, or animal-assisted, therapy, a therapist will introduce an animal into the therapeutic setting. Although the *Journal of the American Medical Association* published a brief report indicating the benefits of pet therapy (Voelker, 1995), few empirical studies exist to validate the positive outcomes typically described in case studies. One study does suggest that pet therapy can convey a number of psychological and physiological benefits, including a decrease in blood pressure, an increase in skin temperature, and a general sense of relaxation (Baun, Oetting, & Bergstrom, 1991). Unfortunately, limited data is available regarding the experience of the participant as well as that of the therapist. Some approaches to pet therapy include goals typically associated with occupational or physical therapy including improvement in balance and bilateral coordination via caregiving for and playing with the animal. Other goals are associated with greater communication sharing via discussing the animal and the child's involvement with it (Velde, Cipriani, & Fisher, 2005).

Art therapy is another adjunctive therapy with various case reports to suggest its effectiveness (Emery, 2004). There is no doubt that children's art and drawings do have meaning, and that they can provide some measure of self-perception, adjustment, and relation to others (e.g., Gardner, 1980). Unfortunately, few studies provide empirical evidence that art therapy promotes specific changes in behavior, communication, or socialization among children suffering from autism (e.g., Hairston, 1990). However, the creativity and sensory integration model approaches to art therapy are consistent with overall occupational therapy goals in that different senses are explored in art therapy through different mediums, and relationships between therapists and children are emphasized. On a case-by-case basis, art therapy may be a positive addition to a child's treatment plan.

Some evidence suggests that individual psychotherapy may be a useful addition to a child's treatment plan (Barrows, 2004; Rhode, 2004). Although the National Institute of Health counsels that using insight-oriented psychotherapy alone is generally ineffective as a treatment for autism (1975), both psychodynamic and cognitive-behavioral approaches may benefit children who have high-functioning autism or Asperger's syndrome. For children who are verbal, and can articulate their internal experience (or experience of being "different" than others), individual psychotherapy may be used to combat anxiety, depression, and obsessive-compulsive symptoms (e.g., Reaven & Hepburn, 2003). Cognitive behavior therapy may benefit such children as they learn to reexamine their expectations and interpretations of external events and others' behavior, and to participate more fully and with flexibility in a constantly changing world. Participation in individual psychotherapy is also empowering because it assumes that children on the spectrum can take an active role in self-assessment and act as their own agents of change.

HOPE FOR THE FUTURE

Children and families affected by autism can also maintain hope for the future. Research on a variety of therapies continues to be conducted, and additional sources of support are often available in the form of grandparents or other extended family members. The field of positive psychology offers a variety of insights into how families can maintain resiliency in spite of significant challenges, and find meaning in their own lives and experiences.

Parents and other nuclear family members coping with autism can certainly use every available social support for coping. One area of potential support typically ignored in the literature is that of grandparents. An initial study of maternal and paternal grandparents of children suffering from autism suggests that grandparents tend to take a more positive view of their grandchild's behavioral symptoms than parents, and that maternal grandmothers appear to provide significantly more emotional support than paternal grandparents (Harris, Handleman, & Palmer, 1985). An important caveat in this area, however, is to acknowledge that, in some cases, grandparental responses to a grandchild's autism can actually represent an additional stressor or burden to parents. Interestingly, a review that examined potential sources of burden suggests that grandparents who refuse to acknowledge their grandchild's disability or diagnosis of autism are regarded as least helpful by parents (Hastings, 1997). This apparent state of denial makes it difficult for parents to successfully implement behavioral treatment in in-vivo situations, such as at home or during visits in the community to the grandparent's home or elsewhere. Some grandparents in denial of their grandchild's disability may also be unavailable to provide necessary emotional support to parents, as well as to the children themselves.

Consider the case of Hunter, a four-year-old boy diagnosed with autism, and his parents Marc and Ellen. Due to a combination of food allergies and colitis, Hunter's diet is quite limited. Hunter is essentially nonverbal and tends to tantrum around meal times and immediately before, and throughout, going to the bathroom. During a visit to his maternal grandparents' home, so that his own parents could go out on a date to dinner, Hunter was given "special treats" by his grandmother that were not allowed in his diet. Upon their return, Hunter's parents noticed the crumbs from a cookie on his shirt and inquired about what Hunter had to eat. Hunter's grandmother retorted, "The boy is so skinny! I don't care what all those fancy doctors say. He needs something to eat to fatten him up. Just look at him! And he sure seemed to like that cookie when I gave it to him!" Needless to say, the evening ended poorly for Marc and Ellen and caused significant damage to their relationship with the grandparents. Hunter himself had some additional stomach distension the following day and tantrummed more at meal time. Hunter's parents felt that they could no longer use Ellen's parents as babysitters and that they had lost one of their primary sources of social support. Ellen and Marc also felt as though their own parents did not trust them as parents, which added further trauma to the experience. Fortunately, after some couple's counseling, Marc and Ellen were able to address the issue with

Hunter's grandparents and explain how important it was that everyone in the family support his treatment. Marc and Ellen also brought over Hunter's X-rays and test results to show Ellen's parents that this was a legitimate medical problem for Hunter and not simply "rigid parenting." When told that they caused their grandchild's stomach pains to worsen after giving Hunter a forbidden food, Ellen's parents apologized profusely and appeared to understand how critical it was to adhere to Hunter's diet. They asked a number of questions about Hunter's test report and explained, "I don't think we ever realized that this was such a big deal ... Now I feel like we know exactly what he can and cannot eat, and why he's so skinny in the first place ... I guess no matter how much food goes in there, only a little bit can get into his system because it's so swollen." More importantly, Ellen's parents realized how their seemingly innocent gesture endangered their relationship as a family, and they were able to tell Ellen and Marc how proud they were of them for taking such good care of Hunter.

This case example supports the few reports available in the literature that suggest that grandparents as a whole want to gain additional information about their grandchild's diagnosis and treatment (Vadasy, Fewell, & Meyer, 1986). Additional concerns that grandparents commonly have about their own, adult child's adjustment to coping with a child suffering from a disability (Gardner, Scherman, Efthimiadis, & Shultz, 2004), which can inhibit or prevent caregiving, may be exacerbated if they are not fully informed about their grandchild's symptoms and treatment. Grandparents themselves may benefit from individual psychotherapy in which they can address their own fears and concerns, and which would better enable them to support their adult children. The stable, supportive role that many grandparents, particularly grandmothers, learn to play in the life of a child suffering from autism (e.g., Findler & Taubman-Ben-Ari, 2003; Siegel, 1996) cannot be underrated. Even if a child's grandparents are geographically distant, they may have the time and personal resources available to engage in advocacy and formal and informal campaigns for making appropriate changes to governmental and institutional policies.

In popular culture, enthusiastic claims are made for the use of laughter within the context of physical and mental health (e.g., laughter is the best medicine.) Some clinicians also feel a similar push to include or emphasize humor within the context of psychotherapy. Considering the extreme stress experienced by families living with autism, one may wonder whether humor should be employed liberally in treatment with affected children and family members. Interestingly, and perhaps unfortunately, empirical research has produced only mixed findings regarding the ability of humor to produce positive health outcomes. Although theories exist that humor and laughter can induce favorable changes to the immune system, empirical studies suggest that such a connection is weak, at best, and that negative emotions, such as fear and disgust, have actually been shown to produce heightened immune function (see Martin, 2001, for a review). Other studies suggest that the effect of humor is more akin to muscle relaxation (Fredrickson, 2000), and can convey an increased tolerance to pain and slight decreases in blood pressure (Martin, 2001). Within the context of psychotherapy, empirical evidence to support the use of humor is limited. An appropriate guideline for clinicians, offered by Saper (1987), may be to employ humor in sessions when it serves a clear purpose, rather than simple comic relief.

RECOVERY, REMISSION, AND RESILIENCY

Significant controversy exists regarding recovery and remission in relation to childhood autism. Some experts argue that autism represents a chronic condition, whereas others assert that the brain is plastic enough to undergo and maintain long-term change. Many therapists find that, with some exceptions, patients and families generally do not focus so much upon the terminology ascribed to these changes, as long as they are positive. Clinicians can also focus on helping children become fully functioning. In accord with the teachings of Carl Rogers (1959), fully functioning individuals accept both their strengths and weaknesses, find purpose and meaning in their lives, develop trusting personal relationships, and are able to receive compassion from others.

It is possible that in order to derive meaning from coping with such a challenging disorder as childhood autism, individuals may make more realistic, yet appropriate, appraisals that include aspects of sadness and wisdom (e.g., Linley, 2003). As stated by one mother of a child suffering from autism, "You know, I love my son so much and he is doing so well, and I really know who we can count on, but I can't help but feel like we've both lost our innocence somewhere along the way. One of my friends actually said to me the other day, 'There is something about Ryan. He is so gentle and somehow seems to know things about other people that I can't quite explain. It's like he is an old man inside a child's body.'"

The emergent field of positive psychology focuses upon health and well-being, as opposed to states of illness and discord. Newer theories proposed within the field, including the organismic valuing theory, suggest that trauma and adversity have the potential to lead to personal growth and meaning in life (Joseph & Linley, 2005). Various studies suggest that many adults who display significant social leadership and creativity share traumatic childhood experiences and difficulty (Simonton, 2000). For both children and affected families, a critical factor in the development of positive outcomes is that of social support and other environmental considerations (Joseph & Linley, 2005). This finding also suggests that advocacy for children and their families, in terms of school support and government funding, becomes essential.

So what is progress in terms of treatment for childhood autism? One father of a five-year-old son on the spectrum remarked, "I now spend my life hoping for the best, but planning for the worst. At least now Brian is talking, and I can say that he actually has two friends at school. He attends typical kindergarten with an aide in the morning, and goes to the resource room for speech and OT in the afternoon. This is a far cry from that one doctor's initial prediction that he would end up in some institution, but we're still not satisfied. And, it's still taking quite a toll on my marriage. I've always got a lot of work to do, if you know what I mean. And we're always looking for the next 'new thing.' And, I still want to know what the hell is going on in his head." And, one father of a three-year-old daughter with autism noted, "Yeah, you really start to find out who your real friends are. They'll invite you over to a picnic at their house even though they know your kid will probably flip out at least once that night ... The counseling also helped my wife and I because it's always been hard for us to ask for help ... And, it was nice to share with someone [our therapist] who really understood how big a deal it was when Katie said her first words. I tell you, as the parent of a child with autism, you don't take anything for granted any more, and everything they do is like a huge gift. I'm starting to see it that way now, and to think about what it's like for my daughter as well."

Although there are no empirical findings to date regarding resiliency among children with autism, a major longitudinal study involving young adults diagnosed with ADHD and other learning disabilities suggests that a number of specific factors contribute to positive outcomes (Werner & Smith, 2001). Resilient children in this study sought personal control over their lives, were willing to seek out support, and were able to identify their areas of strength. Having one significant, positive relationship with an adult who accepted and supported them, such as a parent, coach, or teacher, was associated with better coping and resiliency. The ability to self-regulate or self-soothe has also been implicated as an important factor in resiliency (Masten & Coatsworth, 1998). Thus, children with autism are likely to benefit from interventions that promote self-control and regulation, as well as the ability to advocate for oneself. Again, the role of a supportive, loving adult figure, as well as the child's ability to articulate and enjoy at least one area of personal competence, cannot be understated. Clinicians can certainly assist in this process and help both children and family members affected by autism highlight areas of ability and growth.

There is a need to focus on the quality of life for children on the spectrum, and maintain hope and high standards. For example, it is not enough to allow a child to attend school without an aide. The ultimate goal is for any child to develop an integrated sense of self, a number of mutually satisfying personal relationships, and the ability to live independently. What parent or therapist would not want their child or patient to have friends, find a meaningful career, contribute meaningfully to society, and have a life partner or children if they so choose? In developing and selecting any treatment intervention, pursuing such goals will only add to the requisite sense of urgency, optimism, and entitlement that all children on the spectrum deserve.

Appendix

Links to recommended books, organizations, catalogues, and other resources for information about autism

Books authored by individuals diagnosed with an autism spectrum disorder

Grandin, T. (1995). *Thinking in pictures: And other reports from my life with autism.* New York: Doubleday.

Grandin, T. (1996). *Emergence: Labeled autistic.* New York: Warner.

Jackson, J. (2002). *Freaks, geeks, and Asperger syndrome: A user guide to adolescence.* London: Jessica Kingsley Publishers.

Mukhopadhyay, T. R. (2000). *Beyond the silence: My life, the world, and autism.* London: National Autistic Society. Also published as Mukhopadhyay, T. R. (2003). *The mind tree: A miraculous child breaks the silence of autism.* New York: Arcade Publishing.

Prince-Hughes, D. (Ed.) (2002). *Aquamarine blue: Personal stories of college students with autism.* Athens, OH: Swallow/Ohio University Press.

Shore, S. M. (2003). *Beyond the wall: Personal experiences with autism and Asperger syndrome.* Shawnee Mission, KS: Autism Asperger Publishing Company.

Williams, D. (1992). *Nobody nowhere: The extraordinary autobiography of an autistic.* London: Transworld Publishers.

Williams, D. (2003). *Exposure anxiety: The invisible cage.* London: Jessica Kingsley Publishers.

Informational websites for related organizations and research centers

Action for Autistic Spectrum Disorders (ASD)/UK, www.actionasd.org.uk

Autism Independent UK, www.autismuk.com

Autism Research Institute (ARI), www.autismwebsite.com/ari/dan/dan.htm

Autism Society of America (ASA), www.autism-society.org

Autism Society of Canada (ASC), www.autismsocietycanada.ca/index_e.html

Autistic Society/UK, www.autisticsociety.org

Center for Autism and Related Disorders, Kennedy Krieger Institute at Johns Hopkins University, www.kennedykrieger.org

Center for the Study of Autism (CSA), www.autism.org
Centers for Disease Control (CDC), www.cdc.gov/ncbddd/autism
Children's Hospital of Philadelphia, www.chop.edu/consumer/jsp/division/
generic
Cure Autism Now (CAN), www.cureautismnow.com
Defeat Autism Now! (DAN!), www.autismwebsite.com/ari/dan/whatisdan.htm
First Signs Campaign, www.firstsigns.org
International Autistic Research Organisation, www.charitynet.org/~iaro
National Alliance for Autism Research, www.naar.org
National Autism Society (NAS)/UK, www.nas.org.uk
National Institutes of Health (NIH), www.nih.gov
Parents for the Early Intervention of Autism in Children (PEACH)/UK, www.
peach.org.uk/Home
Public Autism Resource & Information Service (PARIS)/UK, www.info.
autism.org.uk/Pages/Index.aspx
Relationship Development Intervention (RDI), Connections Center, www.
rdiconnect.com/default.asp
SACAR, a charity supporting individuals with Asperger's syndrome and autism/
UK, www.sacar-trust.org
Stroud Autistic Support Group/UK, www.sasg.org.uk
Unlocking Autism, www.unlockingAutism.org
Yale Developmental Disabilities Clinic, http://info.med.yale.edu/chldstdy/autism

Catalogues and suppliers for books, videos, and training materials

Different Roads to Learning (Applied Behavioral Analysis resources and
materials), www.difflearn.com
Future Horizons (autism related books and educational materials), www.
futurehorizons-autism.com
Handwriting without Tears (OT and educational resources), www.hwtears.com
Pocketful of Therapy (OT and educational products), www.pfot.com
Super Dooper Publications (education and speech therapy materials), www.
superduperinc.com
VB Teaching Tools, www.vbteachingtools.com/index.asp

References

Afzal, N., Murch, S., Thirrupathy, K., Berger, L., Fagbemi, A., & Heuschkel, R. (2003). Constipation with acquired megarectum in children with autism. *Pediatrics, 112,* 939–43.

Alderfer, M. A., Kazak, A. E., Cnaan, A., & Annunziato, R. A. (2005). Patterns of PTSD in parents of childhood cancer survivors. *Journal of Family Psychology, 79,* 430–40.

American Psychiatric Association. (2000). *Diagnostic and statistical manual of mental disorders: Text revision* (4th ed.). Washington, DC: APA.

Anderson, S. R., & Romanczyk, R. G. (1999). Early intervention for young children with autism: Continuum-based behavioral models. *Journal of the Association for Persons with Severe Handicaps, 24,* 162–73.

Anonymous. (2002). In D. Prince-Hughes (Ed.), *Aquamarine blue: Personal stories of college students with autism.* Athens, OH: Swallow/Ohio University Press.

Ayers, A. J. (1995). *Sensory integration and the child.* Los Angeles: Western Psychological Services.

Bailey, D. B., Jr., Hatton, D. D., Mesibov, G., Ament, N., & Skinner, M. (2000). Early development, temperament and functional impairment in autism and fragile X syndrome. *Journal of Autism and Developmental Disorders, 30,* 49–59.

Bandura, A. (1971). *Social learning theory.* New York: General Learning Press.

Baron-Cohen, S. (1988). Social and pragmatic deficits in autism: Cognitive or affective? *Journal of Autism and Developmental Disorders, 18,* 379–403.

Baron-Cohen, S., Allen, J., & Gilberg, C. (1992). Can autism be detected at 18 months? The needle, the haystack, and the CHAT. *British Journal of Psychiatry, 161,* 839–43.

Baron-Cohen, S., Ring, H. A., Wheelwright, S., Bullmore, E. T., Brammer, M. J., Simmons, A., & Williams, C. R. (1999). Social intelligence in the normal and autistic brain: An fMRI study. *European Journal of Neuroscience, 11,* 1891–8.

Baron-Cohen, S., & Wheelwright, S. (2004). The empathy quotient: An investigation of adults with Asperger Syndrome or high functioning autism, and normal sex differences. *Journal of Autism and Developmental Disorders, 34,* 163–75.

Barrows, P. (2004). "Playful" therapy: Working with autism and trauma. *International Forum of Psychoanalysis, 13*, 175–86.

Barry, L. M., & Burlew, S. B. (2004). Using Social Stories to teach choice and play skills to children with autism. *Focus on Autism and Other Developmental Disabilities, 19*, 45–52.

Barry, T. D., Klinger, L. G., Lee, J. M., Palardy, N., Gilmore, T., & Bodin. S. D. (2003). Examining the effectiveness of an outpatient clinic-based social skills group for high-functioning children with autism. *Journal of Autism and Developmental Disorders, 33*, 685–701.

Barton, J. S., Cherkasov, M. V., Hefter, R., Cox, T. A., O'Connor, M., & Manoach, D. S. (2004). Are patients with social developmental disorders prosopagnosic? Perceptual heterogeneity in the Asperger and socio-emotional processing disorders. *Brain, 127*, 1706–16.

Bauminger, N., & Kasari, C. (2000). Loneliness and friendship in high-functioning children with autism. *Child Development, 2*, 447–56.

Baun, M. M., Oetting, K., & Bergstrom, N. (1991). Health benefits of companion animals in relation to the physiologic indices of relaxation. *Holistic Nursing Practice, 5*, 16–23.

Bernard, S., Enayati, S., Redwood, L., Roger, H., & Binstock, T. (2001). Autism: A novel form of mercury poisoning. *Medical Hypothesis, 56*, 462–71.

Bitsika, V., & Sharpley, C. F. (2004). Stress, anxiety and depression among parents of children with autism spectrum disorder. *Australian Journal of Guidance & Counselling, 14*, 151–61.

Bondy, A. (2001). PECS: Potential benefits and risks. *The Behavior Analyst Today, 2*, 127–32.

Bondy, A. & Frost, L. (1998). The picture exchange communication system. *Seminars in Speech and Language*, 19, 373–89.

Buitelaar, J. K., Van der Gaag, R., Klin, A., & Volkmar, F. (1999). Exploring the boundaries of Pervasive Developmental Disorder Not Otherwise Specified: Analysis of data from the DSM-IV autistic disorder field trial. *Journal of Autism and Developmental Disorders, 29*, 33–43.

Butnick, S. M. (2005). Neurofeedback in adolescents and adults with attention deficit hyperactivity disorder. *Journal of Clinical Psychology, 61*, 621–5.

Camp, C. J., Cohen-Mansfield, J., & Capezuti, E. A. (2002). Mental health services in nursing homes: Use of nonpharmacologic interventions among nursing home residents with dementia. *Psychiatric Services, 53*, 1397–404.

Carey, D. P. (1996). 'Monkey see, monkey do' cells. *Current Biology, 6*, 1087–8.

Centers for Disease Control and Prevention. (2005). Learn the signs: Act early. Retrieved November 28, 2005 from http://www.cdc.gov/ncbddd/autism/actearly

Chakrabarti, S., & Fombonne, E. (2001). Pervasive developmental disorders in preschool children. *Journal of the American Medical Association, 24*, 3093–9.

Chakrabarti, S., & Fombonne, E. (2005). Pervasive developmental disorders in preschool children: Confirmation of high prevelence. *American Journal of Psychiatry, 162*, 1133–42.

Charlop, M. H., Schreibman, L., & Tyron, A. S. (1983). Learning through observation: The effects of peer modeling on acquisition and generalization in autistic children. *Journal of Abnormal Child Psychology, 11,* 356–66.

Charman, T., Swettenham, J., Baron-Cohen, S., Cox, A., Baird, G., & Drew, A. (1998). An experimental investigation of social-cognitive abilities in infants with autism: Clinical implications. *Infant Mental Health Journal, 19,* 260–75.

Cohen, D. J., & Volkmar, F. R. (Eds.) (1997). *Handbook of autism and pervasive developmental disorders.* New York: Wiley.

Constantino, J. N., Davis, S. A., Todd, R. D., Schindler, M. K., Gross, M. M., Brophy, S. L., Metzger, L. M., Shoushtari, C. S., Splinter, R., & Reich, W. (2003). Validation of a brief quantitative measure of autistic traits: Comparison of the social responsiveness scale with the autism diagnostic interview-revised. *Journal of Autism and Developmental Disorders, 33,* 427–33.

Courchesne, E., Carper, R., & Akshoomoff, N. (2003). Evidence of brain overgrowth in the first year of life in autism. *Journal of the American Medical Association, 290,* 337–44.

Cox, A., Klein, K., Charman, T., Baird, G., Baron-Cohen, S., Swettenham, J., Drew, A., & Wheelwright, S. (1999). Autism spectrum disorders at 20 and 42 months of age: Stability of clinical and ADI-R diagnosis. *Journal of Child Psychology and Psychiatry, 40,* 719–32.

Cunningham, E., & Marcason, W. (2001). Is there any research to support a gluten- and casein-free diet for a child that is diagnosed with autism? *Journal of the American Dietetic Assocation, 101,* 222.

DeMyer, M. K. (1979). *Parents of children with autism.* Wiley: New York.

Dunn, M. E., Burbine, T., Bowers, C. A., & Tantleff-Dunn, S. (2001). Moderators of stress in parents of children with autism. *Community Mental Health Journal, 37,* 39–53.

Eaves, L. C., & Ho, H. H. (2004). The very early identification of autism: Outcome to age 4½–5. *Journal of Autism and Developmental Disorders, 34,* 367–78.

Edelson, S. M., & Rimland, B. (Eds.) (2003). *Treating autism: Parent stories of hope and success.* San Francisco, CA: Autism Research Institute.

Eland, J. (1985). The child who is hurting. *Seminars in Oncology Nursing, 1,* 116–22.

Elkman, P., & Friesen, W. V. (1978). *Facial action coding system, Parts 1 and 2.* San Francisco, CA: University of California, Human Interaction Laboratory.

Elliott, M. R., Fisher, K., & Ames, E. (1988). The effects of rocking on the state and respiration of normal and excessive criers. *Canadian Journal of Psychology, 42,* 163–72.

Emery, M. J. (2004). Art therapy as an intervention for autism. *Art Therapy, 21,* 143–7.

Englemann, S., & Carnine, D. W. (1982). *Theory of instruction: Principles and application.* New York: Irvington.

Erba, H. W. (2000). Early intervention programs for children with autism: Conceptual frameworks for implementation. *American Journal of Orthopsychiatry, 70,* 82–94.

Ernsperger, L., & Stegen-Hansen, T. (2005). *Strategies for addressing eating challenges and food refusal for individuals with ASD.* Paper presented at the annual meeting of the Penn State University Autism Conference, University Park, PA.

Fernandez, E., & Turk, D. C. (1992). Sensory and affective components of pain: Separation and synthesis. *Psychological Bulletin, 112*, 205–17.

Fields, S. A., & Ogles, B. M. (2002). The system of care for children and the least restrictive alternative: Legal origins and current concerns. *Children's Services: Social Policy, Research, and Practice, 5*, 75–93.

Filipek, P. A., Accardo, P. J., Ashwal, S., Baranek, G. T., Cook, E. H. Jr., Dawson, G., Gardon, B., Gravel, J. S., Johnson, C. P., Kallen, R. J., Levy, S. E., Minshew, N. J., Ozonoff, S., Prizant, B. M., Rapin, I., Rogers, S. J., Stone, W. L., Teplin S. W., Tuchman, R. F., & Volkmar, F. R. (2000). Practice parameter: Screening and diagnosis of autism. *Neurology, 55*, 468–79.

Findler, L., & Taubman-Ben-Ari, O. (2003). Social workers' perceptions and practice regarding grandparents in families of children with a developmental disability. *Families in Society, 84*, 86–94.

Fisman, S. N., Wolf, L. C., & Noh, S. (1989). Marital intimacy in parents of exceptional children. *Canadian Journal of Psychiatry, 34*, 519–29.

Fredrickson, B. L. (2000). Cultivating positive emotions to optimize health and well-being. *Prevention and Treatment, 3*, 1–26.

Gardner, H. (1980). *Artful scribbles: The significance of children's drawings.* New York: Basic.

Gardner, J., E., Scherman, A., Efthimiadis, M. S., & Schultz, S. K. (2004). Panamanian grandmothers' family relationships and adjustment to a grandchild with a disability. *International Journal of Aging and Human Development, 59*, 305–20.

Gepner, B., & Mestre, D. (2002). Rapid visual-motion integration deficit in autism. *Trends in Cognitive Science, 6*, 455.

Gilberg, C., & Coleman, M. (1992). *The biology of the autistic syndromes.* London: MacKeith Press.

Gilberg, C., & Coleman, M. (1996). Autism and medical disorders: A review of the literature. *Developmental Medical Child Neurology, 38*, 191–202.

Gladwell, M. (2005). *Blink.* New York: Little, Brown, and Company.

Goin, R. P., & Myers, B. J. (2004). Characteristics of infantile autism: Moving toward earlier detection. *Focus on Autism and Other Developmental Disabilities, 19*, 5–2.

Grandin, T. (1995). *Thinking in pictures: And other reports from my life with autism.* New York: Doubleday.

Gray, C. (1994). The Social Story kit. In C. Gray (Ed.), *The new Social Story book* (pp. 215–44). Arlington, TX: Future Horizons.

Gray, C. (2000). *The new social story book: Illustrated.* Arlington, TX: Future Horizons.

Gray, C., & Gerand, J. (1993). Social Stories: Improving responses of students with autism with accurate social information. *Focus on Autistic Behavior, 8*, 1–10.

Gutstein, S. (2000). *Autism Asperberger's: Solving the relationship puzzle.* Arlington, TX: Future Horizons.

Gutstein, S. E., & Sheely, R. K. (2002). *Relationship development intervention with young children.* London: Jessica Kingsley Publishers.

Gutstein, S E., & Whitney, T. (2002). Asperger syndrome and the development of a social competence. *Focus on Autism and Other Developmental Disorders, 17*, 161–72.

Hairston, M. P. (1990). Analyses of responses of mentally retarded autistic and mentally retarded nonautistic children to art therapy and music therapy. *Journal of Music Therapy, 27,* 137–50.

Haith, M. M. (1990). Progress in the understanding of sensory and perceptual processes in early infancy. *Merrill Palmer Quarterly, 36,* 1–26.

Haith, M. M., Berman, T., & Moore, M. J. (1977). Eye contact and face scanning in early infancy. *Science, 198,* 853–55.

Hamilton, L. M. (2000). *Facing autism: Giving parents reasons for hope and guidance for help.* Colorado Springs, CO: Waterbrook Press.

Harris, S. L., Handleman, J. S., & Palmer, C. (1985). Parents and grandparents view the autistic child. *Journal of Autism and Developmental Disorders, 15,* 127–37.

Hastings, R. P. (1997). Grandparents of children with disabilities: A review. *International Journal of Disability, Development, and Education, 44,* 329–40.

Hastings, R. P. (2003). Behavioral adjustment of siblings of children with autism engaged in applied behavior analysis early intervention programs: The moderating role of social support. *Journal of Autism and Developmental Disorders, 33,* 141–50.

Hatfield, E., Cacioppo, J. T., & Rapson, R. L. (1994). *Emotional contagion.* NY: Cambridge University Press.

Hillman, J. L. (2002). *Crisis intervention and trauma counseling.* New York: Kluwer/Plenum.

Hillman, J. (2006). Supporting and treating families with children on the autistic spectrum: The unique role of the generalist psychologist. *Psychotherapy, 43,* 349–58.

Howlin, P., & Moore, A. (1997). Diagnosis of autism: A survey of over 1200 patients in the UK. *Autism, 1,* 135–62.

Hughes, P. M., & Lieberman, S. (1990). Troubled parents: Vulnerability and stress in childhood cancer. *British Journal of Medical Psychology, 63,* 53–64.

Ivey, M. L., Heflin, L. J., & Alberto, P. (2004). The use of Social Stories to promote independent behaviors in novel events for children with PDD-NOS. *Focus on Autism and Other Developmental Disabilities, 19,* 164–77.

Jackson, L. (2001). *A user's guide to the GF/CF diet for autism, Asperger Syndrome, and AD/HD.* London: Jessica Kingsley Publishers.

Jackson, L. (2002). *Freaks, geeks, & Asperger Syndrome: A user guide to adolescence.* London: Jessica Kingsley Publishers.

James, A., & Barry, R. J. (1980). Respiratory and vascular responses to simple visual stimuli in autistics, retardates, and normals. *Psychophysiology, 17,* 541–7.

Jarusiewicz, B. (2002). Efficacy of neurofeedback for children in the autistic spectrum: A pilot study. *Journal of Neurotherapy, 64,* 39–49.

Johnson, E., & Hastings, R. P. (2002). Facilitating factors and barriers to the implementation of intensive home-based behavioural intervention for young children with autism. *Child: Care, Health, and Development, 28,* 123–30.

Joseph, S., & Linley, P. A. (2005). Positive adjustment to threatening events: An organismic valuing theory of growth through adversity. *Review of General Psychology, 3,* 262–80.

Kalb, C. (2005). When does autism start? *Newsweek, 145*(9), 45–53.

Kaplan, R. S., & Steele, A. L. (2005). An analysis of music therapy program goals and outcomes for clients with diagnoses on the autism spectrum. *Journal of Music Therapy, 42,* 2–19.

Kasari, C., Sigman, M., & Yirmiya, N. (1993). Focused and social attention of autistic children in interactions with familiar and unfamiliar adults: A comparison of autistic, mentally retarded, and normal children. *Development and Psychopathology, 5,* 403–14.

Katz, E. R., Kellerman, J., & Siegal, S. E. (1980). Behavioral distress in children with cancer undergoing medical procedures: Developmental considerations. *Journal of Consulting and Clinical Psychology, 48,* 356–65.

Kennedy, K., & Bachman, J. (1993). Effectiveness of the Lindamood auditory discrimination in depth program with students with learning disabilities. *Learning Disabilities Research and Practice, 8,* 253–9.

Kern, L., Koegel, R. L., Dyer, K., Blew, P. A., & Fenton, L. R. (1982). The effects of physical exercise on self-stimulation and appropriate responding in autistic children. *Journal of Autism and Developmental Disorders, 12,* 399–419.

Klin, A. (2000). Attributing social meaning to ambiguous visual stimuli in higher-functioning autism and Asperger syndrome: The social attribution talk. *Journal of Child Psychology and Psychiatry, 41,* 831–46.

Klin, A., Jones, W., Schultz, R., Volkmar, F., & Cohen, D. (2002). Defining and quantifying the social phenotype in autism. *American Journal of Psychiatry, 159,* 895–908.

Klin, A., Volkmar, F. R., Sparrow, S. S., Cicchetti, D. V., & Rourke, B. P. (1995). Validity and neuropsychological characterization of Asperger syndrome: Convergence with nonverbal learning disabilities syndrome. *Journal of Child Psychology and Psychiatry, 36,* 1127–1240.

Kransny, L., Williams, B. J., Provencal, S., & Ozonoff, S. (2003). Social skills interventions for the autism spectrum: Essential ingredients and a model curriculum. *Child and Adolescent Psychiatric Clinics of North America, 12,* 107–22.

Kuttner, L. (1989). Management of young children's acute pain and anxiety during invasive medical procedures. *Pediatrician, 16,* 39–44.

Laushey, K. M., & Heflin, L. J. (2002). Enhancing social skills of kindergarten children with autism through the training of multiple peers as tutors. *Journal of Autism and Developmental Disorders, 30,* 183–93.

Linley, P. A. (2003). Positive adaptation to trauma: Wisdom as both process and outcome. *Journal of Traumatic Stress, 16,* 601–10.

Lochbaum, M. R., & Crews, D. J. (1995). Exercise prescription for autistic populations. *Journal of Autism and Developmental Disorders, 25,* 335–6.

Loddo, S. (2003). The understanding of actions and intentions in autism. *Journal of Autism and Developmental Disorders, 33,* 545–6.

Lord, C. (1995). Follow-up of two-year-olds referred for possible autism. *Journal of Child Psychology and Psychiatry, 36,* 1365–82.

Lord, C., Risi, S., Lambrecht, L., Cook, E. H. Jr., Leventhal, B. L., DiLavore, P. C., Pickles, A., & Rutter, M. (2000). The Autism Diagnostic Observation Schedule Generic: A standard measure of social and communication deficits associated with the spectrum of autism. *Journal of Autism and Developmental Disorders, 30,* 205–23.

Lord, C., Rutter, M., & LeCouteur, A. (1994). Autism Diagnostic Interview – Revised: A revised version of a diagnostic interview for caregivers of individuals with possible pervasive developmental disorders. *Journal of Autism and Developmental Disorders, 24,* 659–85.

Lovaas, O. I. (1987). Behavioural treatment and normal educational and intellectual functioning in young autistic children. *Journal of Consulting and Clinical Psychology, 28,* 3–9.

Lovaas, O. I., Smith, T., & McEachin, J. J. (1989). Clarifying comments on the young autism study: Reply to Schopler, Short, and Mesibov. *Journal of Consulting and Clinical Psychology, 37,* 165–7.

Lubar, J. F. (1995). Neurofeedback for the management of attention deficit hyperactivity disorders. In M. S. Schwartz (Ed.), *Biofeedback: A practitioner's guide* (pp. 493–522). New York: Guilford.

Luscre, D. M., & Center, D. B. (1996). Procedures for reducing dental fear in children with autism. *Journal of Autism and Developmental Disorders, 26,* 547–56.

MacLaren, J. E., & Cohen, Lindsey. (2005). Teaching behavioral pain management to healthcare professionals: A systematic review of research in training programs. *Journal of Pain, 6,* 481–92.

Marshall, R. S., Lazar, R. M., Binder, J. R., Desmond, D. W., Drucker, P. M., & Mohr, J. P. (1994). Intrahemispheric localization of drawing dysfunction. *Neuropsychologia, 32,* 493–501.

Martin, R. A. (2001). Humor, laughter, and physical health: Methodological issues and research findings. *Psychological Bulletin, 127,* 504–19.

Masten, A. S., & Coatsworth, J. D. (1998). The development of competence in favorable and unfavorable environments: Lessons on successful children. *American Psychologist, 53,* 205–20.

Matson, J. L., & Love, S. R. (1990). A comparison of parent-reported fear for autistic and nonhandicapped age-matched children and youth. *Australia & New Zealand Journal of Developmental Disabilities, 16,* 349–53.

McAffe, J. (2001). *Navigating the social world.* Future Horizons: Arlington, TX.

McCandless, J. (2003). *Children with starving brains: A medical treatment guide for autism spectrum disorder.* Canada: Bramble.

McEachin, J. J., Smith, T., & Lovaas, O. I. (1993). Long-term outcome for children with autism who received early intensive behavioural treatment. *American Journal on Mental Retardation, 28,* 359–72.

McGrath, P. A., & Unruh, A. M. (1988). *Pain in children and adolescents: Pain research and clinical management.* Amsterdam: Elsevier.

Melmed, R. D., Schneider, C. K., Fabes, R. A., Phillips, J., & Reichelt, K. (2000). Metabolic markers and gastrointestinal symptoms in children with autism and related disorders. *Journal of Pediatric Gastroenterology and Nutrition, 31,* S31–32.

Melzak, R., & Wall, P. D. (1965). Pain mechanisms: A new theory. *Science, 150,* 971–78.

Monastra, V. J., Lubar, J. F., & Linden, M. (2001). The development of a quantitative electroencephalographic scanning process for attention deficit-hyperactivity disorder: Reliability and validity studies. *Neuropsychology, 15,* 136–44.

Monastra, V. J., Lubar, J. R., Linden, M., VanDeusen, P., Green, G., Wing, W.,

Phillips, A. & Fenger, T. N. (1999). Assessing attention deficit hyperactivity disorder via quantitative electroencephalography: An initial validation study. *Neuropsychology, 13,* 424–33.

Monastra, V. J., Lynn, S., Linden, M., Lubar, J. F., Gruzelier, J., & LaVaque, T. (2005). Electroencephalographic biofeedback in the treatment of Attention Deficit/Hyperactivity Disorder. *Applied Psychophysiology and Biofeedback, 30,* 95–114.

Morgan, S. (1988). Diagnostic assessment of autism: A review of objective scales. *Journal of Psychoeducational Assessment, 6,* 139–51.

National Institute of Health (1975). *Research in the service of mental health.* Rockville, MD: National Institute of Health.

Noens, I. L., van Berckelaer, O., & Ina, A. (2005). Captured by details: Sense-making, language and communication in autism. *Journal of Communication Disorders, 38,* 123–41.

Oberman, L. M., Hubbard, E. M., McCleery, J. P., Altschuler, E. L., Ramachandran, V. S., & Pineda, J. A. (2005). EEG evidence for mirror neuron dysfunction in autism spectrum disorders. *Cognitive Brain Research, 24,* 190–8.

Obler, L. K., & Fein, D. (Eds.) (1988). *The exceptional brain: Neuropsychology of talent and special abilities.* New York: Guilford.

Okuda, K., & Inoue, M. (2000). A behavior analytic view of teaching "theory of mind" to children with autism: Stimulus control and generalization on false belief tasks. *Japanese Psychological Review, 43,* 427–42.

O'Neill, R., Horner, R., Albin, R., Sprague, J., Storey, K., & Newton, J. (1997). *Functional assessment and program development for problem behavior.* 2nd Ed. New York: Brooks/Cole.

Partington, J. W., & Sundberg, M. L. (1998). *The assessment of basic language and learning skills: An assessment, curriculum guide, and tracking system for children with autism or other developmental disabilities.* Danville, CA: Behavior Analysts, Inc.

Patterson, K., & Klopovich, P. M. (1987). *Pain in the pediatric oncology patient: Cancer pain management.* New York: Grune & Stratton.

Perner, J., Frith, J., Leslie, A. M., & Leekman, S. R. (1989). Exploration of the autistic child's theory of mind: Knowledge, belief and communication. *Child Development, 60,* 589–700.

Perry, A. (1991). Rett syndrome: A comprehensive review of the literature. *American Journal on Mental Retardation, 96,* 275–90.

Pilowsky, T., Yirmiva, N., Doppelt, P. O., Gross-Tsur, V., & Shalev, R. S. (2004). Social and emotional adjustment of siblings of children with autism. *Journal of Child and Clinical Psychology and Psychiatry, 45,* 855–65.

Prince-Hughes, D. (Ed.) (2002). *Aquamarine blue: Personal stories of college students with autism.* Athens, OH: Swallow/Ohio University Press.

Rapin, I. (1997). Autism. *The New England Journal of Medicine, 337,* 97–105.

Reaven, J., & Hepburn, S. (2003). Cognitive-behavioral treatment of obsessive-compulsive disorder in a child with Asperger syndrome: A case report. *Autism, 7,* 145–64.

Rhode, M. (2004). Different responses to trauma in two children with autistic spectrum disorder: The mouth as crossroads for the sense of self. *Journal of Child Psychotherapy, 30,* 3–20.

Rizzolatti, C., Camarda, R., Gallese, V., & Fogassi, L. (1995). Premotor cortext and the recognition of motor actions. *Cognitive Brain Research, 3,* 131–41.

Robbins, J. (2000). *A symphony in the brain: The evolution of the new brain wave biofeedback.* New York: Atlantic Monthly Press.

Robins, D. I., Fein, D., Barton, M. I., & Green, J. A. (2001). The modified checklist for autism in toddlers: An initial study investigating the early detection of autism and pervasive developmental disorders. *Journal of Autism and Developmental Disorders, 31,* 131–44.

Rodrique, J. R., Morgan, S. B., & Geffken, G. (1990). Families of autistic children: Psychological functioning of mothers. *Journal of Clinical Child Psychology, 19,* 371–9.

Rogers, C. (1959). A theory of therapy, personality and interpersonal relationships, as developed in the client-centered framework. In S. Koch (Ed.), *Psychology: A study of a science: Vol. 3. Formulations of the person and the social context* (pp. 184–256). New York: McGraw-Hill.

Rowe, C. (1999). Do Social Stories benefit children with autism in mainstream primary schools? *British Journal of Special Education, 26,* 12–14.

Rutherford, M. D., & Rogers, S. J. (2003). Cognitive underpinnings of pretend play in autism. *Journal of Autism and Developmental Disorders, 33,* 289–301.

Rutter, M., Bailey, A., & Lord, C. (2005). *Social communication questionnaire.* Los Angeles: Western Psychological Services.

Sabbagh, M. A. (2004). Understanding orbitofrontal contributions to theory of mind reasoning: Implications for autism. *Brain and Cognition, 55,* 209–19.

Sacks, O. (1995). *An anthropologist on Mars.* New York: Knopf.

Sansosti, F. J., Powell-Smith, K. A., & Kincaid, D. (2004). A research synthesis of Social Story interventions for children with autism spectrum disorders. *Focus on Autism and Other Developmental Disabilities, 19,* 194–205.

Saper, B. (1987). Humor in psychotherapy: Is it good or bad for the client? *Professional Psychology: Research and Practice, 18,* 360–7.

Scattone, D., Wilczynski, S. M., Edwards, R. P., & Rabian, B. (2002). Decreasing disruptive behaviours of children with autism using social stories. *Journal of Autism and Developmental Disorders, 32,* 535–43.

Schall, C. (2000). Family perspectives on raising a child with autism. *Journal of Child and Family Studies, 9,* 409–23.

Schooler, J. W., Ohlsson, S., & Brooks, K. (1993). Thoughts beyond words: When language overshadows insight. *Journal of Experimental Psychology, 122,* 166–83.

Schopler, E., & Olley, J. G. (1982). Comprehensive educational services for autistic children: The TEACCH model. In C. R. Reynolds and T. R. Gutkin (Eds.), *The handbook of school psychology* (pp. 626–43). New York: Wiley.

Schopler, E., Reichler, R., & Rochen-Renner, B. (1988). *The Childhood Autism Rating Scale.* Los Angeles, CA: Western Psychological Services.

Schreck, K. A., Mulick, J. A., & Smith, A. F. (2004). Sleep problems as possible predictors of intensified symptoms of autism. *Research in developmental disabilities, 25,* 57–66.

Shea, V. (2004). A perspective on the research literature related to early intensive behavioral intervention (Lovaas) for young children with autism. *Autism, 8,* 349–67.

Sherer, M. R., & Schreibman, L. (2005). Individual behavioral profiles and predictors of treatment effectiveness for children with autism. *Journal of Consulting and Clinical Psychology, 73,* 525–38.

Shore, S. M. (2005). *Living with autistic spectrum disorder: Professional and personal perspectives.* Paper presented at the National Autism Conference, University Park, PA.

Shreeve, J. (2005). Beyond the brain. *National Geographic, 207,* 2–29.

Sichel, A. G., Fehmi, L. G., & Goldstein, D. M. (1995). Positive outcome with neurofeedback treatment in a case of mild autism. *Journal of Neurotherapy, 11,* 60–64.

Siegel, B. (1996). *The world of the autistic child: Understanding and treating autistic spectrum disorders.* Oxford, England: Oxford University Press.

Sigman, M., & Capps, L. (1997). *Children with autism: A developmental perspective.* Cambridge, MA: Harvard University Press.

Sigman, M., & Ruskin, E. (1999). Continuity and change in social competence of children with autism, Down Syndrome, and developmental delays. *Monographs of the Society for Research in Child Development, 64,* v–114.

Sigman, M., Ungerer, J., Mundy, P., & Sherman, T. (1986). Cognition in autistic children. In D. J. Cohen, A. M. Donnellen, & R. Paul (Eds.), *Handbook of autism and pervasive developmental disorders* (pp. 103–20). New York: Wiley.

Simonton, D. K. (2000). The positive repercussions of traumatic events and experiences: The life lessons of historic geniuses. In P. A. Linley (Ed.), *Psychological trauma and its positive adaptations* (pp. 21–23). Leicester, England: British Psychological Society.

Smith, B., Chung, M. C., & Vostanis, P. (1994). The path to care in autism: Is it better now? *Journal of Autism and Developmental Disorders, 24,* 551–63.

Smith, C. (2001). Using Social Stories to enhance behaviour in children with autistic spectrum difficulties. *Educational Psychology in Practice, 17,* 337–45.

Smith, T. (1999). Outcome of early intervention for children with autism. *Clinical Psychology: Science and Practice, 6,* 33–49.

Solomon, H., Solomon, L. Z., Arnone, M. M., Maur, B. J., Reda, R. M., & Rother, E. O. (1981). Anonymity and helping. *Journal of Social Psychology, 113,* 37–43.

Solomon, M., Goodlin-Jones, B. L., & Anders, T. F. (2004). A social adjustment enhancement intervention for high functioning autism, Asperger's Syndrome, and Pervasive Developmental Disorder NOS. *Journal of Autism and Developmental Disorders, 34,* 649–68.

Strain, S., & Schwartz, I. (2001). ABA and the development of meaningful social relations for young children with autism. *Focus on Autism and Other Developmental Disabilities, 16,* 120–8.

Striano, T., & Berlin, E. (2005). Coordinated affect with mothers and stranger: A longitudinal analysis of joint engagement between 5 and 9 months of age. *Cognition and Emotion, 19,* 781–90.

Strock, Margaret (2004). *Autism spectrum disorders.* (NIH Publication No. NIH-04-5511). Bethesda, MD: National Institutes of Health.

Sundberg, M. L., & Partington, J. W. (1998). *Teaching language to children with autism or other developmental disabilities.* Danille, CA: Behavior

Analysts, Inc.

Taylor, S. J. (2004). Caught in the continuum: A critical analysis of the principle of the least restrictive environment. *Research and Practice for Persons with Severe Disabilities, 29,* 218–30.

Thompson, L. (2002). *Helping autistic spectrum disorders.* Paper presented at the annual meeting of the Society for Neuronal Regulation, Scottsdale, AZ.

Thompson, L., & Thompson, M. (1998). Neurofeedback combined with metacognitive strategies: Effectiveness with students with ADD. *Applied Physiology and Biofeedback, 23,* 243–63.

Thompson, M., & Thompson, L. (2003). *The neurofeedback book: An introduction to basic concepts in applied psychophysiology.* Wheat Ridge, CO: Association for Applied Psychophysiology.

Tidmarsh, L., & Volkmar, F. R. (2003). Diagnosis and epidemiology of autism spectrum disorders. *Canadian Journal of Psychiatry, 48,* 517–25.

Tronick, E., Als, H., Adamsen, L., Wise, S., & Brazelton, T. (1978). The infant's response to entrapment between contradictory messages in face to face interaction. *Journal of the American Academy of Child Psychiatry, 17,* 1–11.

Tuchman, R. F., & Rapin, I. (1997). Regression in pervasive developmental disorders: Seizures and epileptiform electroencephalogram correlates. *Pediatrics, 99,* 560–6.

Vadasy, P. F., Fewell, R. R., & Meyer, D. J. (1986). Grandparents of children with special needs: Insights into their experiences and concerns. *Journal of the Division of Early Childhood, 10,* 36–44.

Velde, B. P., Cipriani, J., Fisher, G. (2005). Resident and therapist views of animal-assisted therapy: Implications for occupational therapy practice. *Australian Occupational Therapy Journal, 52,* 43–50.

Voelker, R. (1995). Puppy love can be therapeutic, too. *Journal of the American Medical Association, 274,* 1897.

Volkmar, F. R., & Nelson, D. S. (1990). Seizure disorders in autism. *Journal of the American Academy of Child and Adolescent Psychiatry, 29,* 127–9.

Volkmar, F. R., & Wiesner, L. A. (2004). *Healthcare for children on the autism spectrum: A guide to medical, nutritional, and behavioral issues.* Bethesda, MD: Woodbine House.

Vostanis, P., Smith, B., Corbett, J., Sungum-Paliwal, R., Edwards, A., Gingell, K., Golding, R., Moore, A., & Williams, J. (1998). Parental concerns of early development in children with autism and related disorders. *Autism, 2,* 229–42.

Werner, E. E., & Smith, R. S. (2001). *Journeys from childhood to midlife.* Ithaca, NY: Cornell University Press.

Whipple, J. (2004). Music in intervention for children and adolescents with autism: A meta-analysis. *Journal of Music Therapy, 41,* 90–106.

Williams, D. (2003). *Exposure anxiety: The invisible cage.* London, England: Jessica Kingsley Publishers.

Williams, E. (2004). Who really needs a "theory" of mind? An interpretive phenomenological analysis of the autobiographical writings of ten high-functioning individuals with an autism spectrum disorder. *Theory and Psychology, 14,* 704–24.

Williams, J. H., Whiten, A., Suddendorf, T., & Perrett, D. I. (in press). Imitation, mirror neurons, and autism. *Neuroscience and Biobehavioral Reviews.*

Winnicott, D. W. (1951). Transitional objects and transitional phenomena. In D. Winnicott (Ed.), *Through paediatrics to psychoanalysis* (pp. 229–42). New York: Basic.

Wolf, N. S., Gales, M. E., Shane, E., & Shane, M. (2001). The developmental trajectory from amodal perception to empathy and communication: The role of mirror neurons in this process. *Psychoanalytic Inquiry, 21*, 94–112.

Index